THE FURIOUS
SOUND
OF GLORY

THE FURIOUS
SOUND
OF GLORY

UNLEASHING HEAVEN ON EARTH
THROUGH A SUPERNATURAL GENERATION

JEFF JANSEN

Published and distributed by Global Fire Creations – www.globalfirecreations.com

Cover design: C. Rayne Warne – rayne@globalfireministries.com
Page design: Mark Buschgens – www.markedbydesign.net

For additional copies of this book and other resources by Jeff Jansen, contact Global Fire Creations by phone: 1 (615) 867-1124 or by email: info@globalfirecreations.com

Printed and Manufactured in the United States

ISBN 13: 978-0-9851128-0-6

DEDICATION

I want to dedicate this book to my wife Jan, who is my best friend, partner in ministry and absolute love of my life. Without your support and understanding of what it takes for me to do what I do, most of the ministry, including my writing, would not be possible. Time and time again you have set your own needs aside to put others first without ever complaining, and doing so with a pure heart and not begrudgingly. You are a true treasure to me and are the glue that holds this whole thing together. Not only is Jan the mother of our seven, soon to be eight children, but she is a grandparent along with myself to ten grand kids—which I'm sure there will be many, many more to come. I love you baby!

Jeff Jansen

ACKNOWLEDGEMENTS

I want to acknowledge all those that have worked so hard on this project to make it a reality. I want to thank Julia Loren for her contribution in editing along with Matt Clyde and Paula Roth for the hours of research, transcription and information of many of my messages. Thank you all.

ENDORSEMENTS

The Furious Sound of Glory is a wonderful book. The author, Jeff Jansen, has done a great job of helping us understand the connection between the visible and invisible world, between the natural and the spiritual. This will surely be used as a textbook for a hungry generation looking for instruction on how to shape the course of world history.

Bill Johnson
Author, *When Heaven Invades Earth*, and *Essential Guide to Healing*
Senior pastor, Bethel Church, Redding, CA

Brilliant! *The Furious Sound of Glory* is a great addition to the arsenal of weapons available today to help unleash Heaven on Earth through the Spirit of Revival. Jeff Jansen is an Apostolic voice and present day revivalist who carries a timely word for the worship, presence and supernatural moves of the Holy Spirit in the earth today. Excellent!

James W. Goll
Encounters Network • Prayer Storm • Compassion Acts
Best Selling Author in the Global Prayer and Prophetic Movement

Jeff Jansen has tapped into the very heart of God for this new epoch season. *The Furious Sound of Glory* unearths a "new sound" for a new season. This book is a clarion call for radical revivalists to rise up in this epic transition and take our rightful place on earth. Jeff is like a Holy Spirit conductor, leading the armies of God into a new song of revelation, and unleashing the heavenly realms to reign until all flesh is drenched with the outpouring of God's Spirit. I highly recommend *The Furious Sound of Glory*.

Kris Vallotton
Co-Founder of Bethel School of Supernatural Ministry
Author of seven books including, *The Supernatural Ways of Royalty*
Senior Associate Leader of Bethel Church, Redding, California

For over the last four years I've worked closely with Jeff Jansen, a present day general in the Body of Christ, and a good friend and mentor of mine. I've been continually amazed by his hunger, passion and faith to see and release the supernatural exploits of God and to train and equip this generation to move in miracle working power. In his book, *The Furious Sound of Glory*, Jeff Jansen describes and has prophesied about this next great awakening—It's time to harmonize with heaven's heartbeat and release on the earth *The Furious Sound of Glory!*

Eric Green
Overseer, Global Fire School of Supernatural
Ministry & Kingdom Life Institute
Global Fire Church & World Miracle Center

The Furious Sound of Glory by Jeff Jansen will deeply stir your heart and set your soul ablaze for more of God's Glory and power to be released upon the earth. Jeff releases insights that will help prepare you to be true overcomers. You will gain valuable insights into the spiritual significance of both sights and sounds. This book will help awaken your heart to seek the Lord on a much higher level. I recommend this book without any hesitation.

Bobby Conner
Eagles View Ministries

Over the last several years I have observed the Lord doing extraordinary things in and through the life and ministry of Jeff Jansen. With his new book, *The Furious Sound of Glory*, Jeff once again taps into God's blueprint for this day with accuracy and relevance for the 21st century overcoming Army of God. The spiritual significance of both light and sound have always fascinated me, particularly during intervals of spiritual outpouring and revival. Clearly, our realms of understanding will go to much greater heights involving throne room activity where the apostle John describes incredible displays of God's nature and power. As the Scripture declares, "He that hath an ear, let him hear what the Spirit is saying." The book that you now hold in your hand will certainly help you in that lofty endeavor.

Paul Keith Davis
WhiteDove Ministries

My friend, Jeff Jansen, inspires us with yet another great book. His passion for God's glory will stir your heart with a fresh desire for the supernatural. An insightful work that is readable, practicable, yet deeply rooted in the revelatory realm. Absolutely, a must read!

Larry Randolph
Larry Randolph Ministries

In his new book, *The Furious Sound of Glory*, Jeff Jansen gives an invitation to the body of Christ to prepare themselves for what is coming in this season. We're in a time of equipping and preparation for new realms of the supernatural. Jeff's vivid insight will give you greater understanding of the times ahead. I believe this book will be profitable to gain greater understanding of what is coming from heaven to earth.

Bob Jones
Bob Jones Ministries

Many religious institutions have missed very real and valid visitations by closing their doors to anything that challenges their experience. We as Christians are also known to resist any experience or theology that was not initiated within our group or movement. It is also true that many of our past experiences serve to keep us from embracing what God desires to do in our future. Basically, we become so full of what God said, that we can't hear what God is saying. And, we feel that we have an obligation to God to resist anything that challenges the sanctity of our present theology.... Well, prepare to be challenged as you read this book by Jeff Jansen.

Ray Hughes
Selah Ministries

I believe that God is releasing a new sound in this generation that carries revival fire and passionate intimacy. It comes in music, prayer, preaching, and the prophetic but it is rooted in a deep love for Jesus, the pursuit of the knowledge of God, and radical holiness. You will enjoy this book by Jeff Jansen and I pray it becomes a catalyst to releasing your own sound.

Jake Hamilton
Jesus Culture Artist

This amazing book is filled with incredible revelation that will propel you into a greater understanding of the Kingdom of God. It also parallels the powerful, miracle producing life of Jeff Jansen and echoes the anointing of what is being released in the earth today. Your life will change as you read this phenomenal revelation!

Dr. Larry Lea, PhD
Best-selling author and father of the present day
international prayer movement

CONTENTS

FORWARD
BY MAHESH CHAVDA

A few years ago the congregation in Charlotte that Bonnie and I pastor had outgrown our auditorium. We set up a large tent on our property and started worshiping in this tabernacle. One evening in the midst of more than a thousand people I felt led to stand up and sing. The song came from 2 Corinthians 3:17-18, "Now the Lord is the Spirit, and where the Spirit of the Lord is there is Liberty, Liberty, Liberty." Suddenly, in the middle of the tent a glorious cloud with golden light appeared. People rose up pointing to the cloud. It was an amazing manifestation that is hard to describe in human language. It hovered over us for more than thirty minutes, and a sense of awe came over all of us. That cloudy Presence hovered not only in the tent, but was visible above the tent, too.

I recall the previous time I had been completely overwhelmed by this cloud of glory. Some years before at noonday in a crowd of 30,000 people in Kinshasa, the Congo, that manifestation resulted in the resurrection of a six-year-old boy named Katshinyi. At the same time that cloud in Kinshasa connected with my dying son, Aaron, born prematurely and barely breathing in the ICU in South Florida, and healed him completely. I knew it was the cloud of glory that made all the difference. Since then, I have witnessed countless healings and miracles over the years, and I always point to the cloud of glory, the thick manifestation of the Holy Spirit, giving all praise to our Lord and Master, Jesus Christ.

But how does this happen? There are few men I know who can explain this wonderful mystery. But my friend Jeff Jansen is one of them. He passionately loves the glory presence that comes in the name of Jesus. If you want to relate to the wonderful glory of Christ, this book is one of the precious treasures that will help you come in harmony with the presence of the glory.

Do you know that God sang creation into being? Do you know how to come into alignment with the sound of glory? Do you know how light and sound relate with God's presence. I could literally sit for days listening to someone who has insight into this unique, glorious realm. In this hour, Jeff Jansen relates to this realm like few others.

Now is the time for all believers to have a deeper revelation of the glory and riches of the Lamb of God. According to Isaiah 60, in the last days we are to arise and shine with the glory of the Lord. This is imperative so that the nations can come to the brightness of the shining of the light, receiving salvation.

I have had wonderful times fellowshipping with Jeff and his precious family. He is a humble man, completely enamored with God's glory. I love comparing notes with him. I can assure you of this: He's a man in harmony with this glory presence. I believe this is a book you will come back to over and over. Each time you do, you will glean more insight into the glory realm.

This is a strategic hour in which God wants to pour out His spirit of revival with signs and wonders in every nation. I sincerely believe the key is the glory presence.

My prayer is God will use *The Furious Sound of Glory* to assist every believer desiring to be used by God in the last days. Stay hungry. Stay humble. And watch God's glory do mighty things.

Mahesh Chavda
Senior Pastor, All Nations Church

Chapter 1

IN THE BEGINNING GOD SANG

In *The Chronicles of Narnia,* by C.S. Lewis, *Aslan* the Lion tells the story of creation to the Lord Adam and Lady Eve. Narnia is amazing with its huge icy mountains, waterfalls, rivers and giant forests. However, the power of the white witch kept the land of Narnia and all its inhabitants frozen and asleep for a long time. Many people had been turned to stone by the spell of the white witch. Suddenly, Aslan roars. They wake up and come back to life as Aslan releases his breath over them. Instantly, the landscape is transformed by the sound of His roar. Color invades and restores the hills and valleys and the mountains spring to life once again revealing His true nature.

The sound of the roar of the Lion of the Tribe of Judah is being released upon this generation. It will change and restore everything it touches right down to the core structure or subatomic level. Every generation from the beginning of time also contained its own sound. Once released, the Roar of the Lord shattered the opposition, unfroze the inhabitants of the land, and turned hearts of stone into flesh and blood. That sound created breakthrough, which enabled the transformation of the regions in which they lived, revealing the intentions and purposes of God. Now, in our time, a generation must arise and wake up from its slumber to release the fresh new sound of heaven. Even creation itself will respond to the sound of heaven on earth with rumblings, quakings and shakings.

In the end, Aslan would lay his life down for the fallen sons of Adam to restore them to their place as lords of creation, kings of the earth. And as it was for Aslan and the inhabitants of Narnia, so it is for us. It took the death of Jesus Christ, the One True Heavenly King, to restore us to our rightful place as kings and lords of the earth. It was for the joy that was set before Him, that He endured the cross, knowing that on the other side of the pain there would be you and I, the redeemed sons and daughters of the Heavenly King. His intention is that the on true "Heavenly King" (Jesus) would live through the many kings on the earth and establish His reign of authority through a family. So, in this final chapter of human history and on this side of eternity, The Lion of the Tribe of Judah is roaring again, unleashing the furious sound of heaven on the earth through an end time army of God.

The final chapter of these events will be so terrible, so incredible in the earth, that even the elements will shudder with great shaking as angels and demons wage war in the heavenly realm. Intercession will focus on the arrival and coming forth of a Kingdom family who is filled with the sound of His roar. They will have power and authority to manifest the Glory of God in the Earth, breaking the curse over creation and releasing healing in the nations, causing them to flourish once again in the glorious freedom for which they were created.

Some would say this is too far reaching and are but visions of grandeur! When in reality these scriptural truths are yet to be apprehended and walked out by a Supernatural Church, the "called out ones" or the "ecclesia." This company of believers will reach far beyond the normative mindsets of the day and demonstrate the miraculous in ways not seen in church history. Jesus Christ paid the ultimate price in blood through Calvary to open the heavens and restore to us the Keys to the Kingdom. He will reap the reward of His suffering.

Even now, the clash between heaven and earth is mounting. Darkness is become increasingly dark and powerful as we draw near to the end and towards the Great Revival. The church is under pressure and is being squeezed to produce the sweet wine of heaven. There are great pressures in the earth and pressure in the heavens. Cosmic violence is beginning to spill out upon the earth. Heaven is not for the faint of heart but is a violent realm causing even the strongest to fear and tremble. This heavenly fury will be poured out in these last days upon an end time Army of God that has been prepared to carry it. And this Army will unleash the Spirit of Revival in the nations of the earth.

We must get ready for the unleashing of the furious sound of Glory—the roar of power and love that transforms the earth.

THE END WILL LOOK LIKE THE BEGINNING

Can you imagine what it must have been like in the beginning of time, before the fall of Adam? It was a world that was beautiful and existed in perfect harmony with God and man. Can you imagine what it must have been like as the worlds were being tethered together and creation was being fashioned by the hand of God? What an awesome thing to think about.

I love to watch the History channel when I'm home, in particular the shows about the earth's formation and position in the galaxy. Science is baffled by the galaxies and planetary systems and how intricately it all works as a gigantic timing mechanism spinning through space. All of it is so incredible and wonderful that it simply baffles the mind. But how did it all come into existence? Science has one theory, but Scripture tells the truth. We know that Genesis 1:3 reads:

> IN THE *beginning God (prepared, formed, fashioned, and) created the heavens and the earth. The earth was without form and an empty waste, and darkness was upon the face of the very great deep. The Spirit of God was moving (hovering, brooding) over the face of the waters. And God said, Let there be light; and there was light.*

We see here that there is a formula for Creation. The first thing we see is that in the beginning God prepared, formed, fashioned, and created the heavens and the earth. The earth had no form and was an "empty waste" with darkness upon the face of the deep. There was something there before God spoke! Some believe that the earth was literally in a place of being "re-created" because Chaos was already in the world and that there was a war over the territory of earth and a pre-Adamic race of man that Satan had already corrupted. But because there is not enough in Scripture to conclusively point in that direction we must stick with what we do know. The earth was there already but "had no form" and that "darkness was upon the face of the deep." There was no natural sun as of yet and everything was in complete darkness.

The second thing we see is that the Spirit of God was moving, hovering, and brooding over the face of the waters. The Holy Spirit of God, like creative DNA, hovered over the face of the waters as there was no land mass on this formless earth at this point. The Holy Spirit is the creative nature and power of the Godhead. He is seen here in Genesis 1:1-3 as an intricate participant in the history of creation. He is moving, scanning, brooding. 2 Chronicles 16:9 reads:

> *For the eyes of the Lord run to and fro throughout the whole earth to show Himself strong in behalf of those whose hearts are blameless toward Him.*

The Holy Spirit was scanning back and forth over the earth in creation as well. He (the Holy Spirit) is what the Scripture calls the *Eyes of the Lord, The Seven Eyes, or Flames, or the Seven-fold Holy Spirit of God* in Revelation 1 that are constantly scanning, testing, searching and hovering over creation.

Thirdly, we see that God spoke and said, "Let there be light," and there was light. Remember the sun and moon were not created until the fourth day so there was no natural light created yet. This light was the Light of the

Glory of God. Although light and sound are located on different frequencies, they are the same thing. Scripture states that "God is Light" and that everything that God has ever brought forth has come from the creative "Voice of the Lord." It was not the natural light that came first, it was the Glory Light.

SOUND AND LIGHT SPECTRUM

When the climate or conditions were right God "Spoke," He "Commanded," He "Decreed" and it was established. Many Hebrew scholars believe that when God spoke the worlds into being in Genesis 1, that He actually *sang* creation into existence. His Voice was a song that sang, "Let there be light" and there was light. The day God chose to create light was the day music began.

In Ray Hughes' book *Sound of Heaven, Symphony of Earth* he says, "Light and sound travel through the medium of waves. Moving light waves are called electromagnetic waves, which determine what type of light it is. As humans, we're only able to see 3 percent of the entire light spectrum, and part of the 97 percent of invisible light is categorized as electromagnetic light. Within electromagnetic light exists a range of wavelengths called "radio waves." Within this category of radio waves exists an even smaller range of waves that humans can hear. Essentially, we know that all these categories and forms of light and sound exist within the same spectrum. So the first time God said, "Let there be light," He was also proclaiming the beginning of sound and music."[1]

Can you imagine what it would be like if you could hear God singing? Remember that it was merely a spoken word that brought the universe into existence. What would happen if God lifted up his voice and not only spoke but sang! Perhaps a new heaven and a new earth would be created. God says something almost just to that effect in Isaiah 65:17-18,

Behold, I create a new heavens and a new earth... I create Jerusalem to be a rejoicing, and her people a joy.

When God spoke at the beginning, the heavens and the earth were created. Perhaps at the end, the new heavens and the new earth will be created when God exults over his people with loud singing.

When I think of the voice of God singing, I hear the booming of Niagara Falls mingled with the trickle of a mountain stream. I hear the blast of Mt. St. Helens mingled with the sound of a baby sleeping. I hear the power of an East Coast hurricane and the gentle wind of a winter snow in Wisconsin. I can hear the unimaginable roar of the sun 865,000 miles thick, one million three hundred thousand times bigger than the earth, and nothing but fire... 1,000,000 degrees centigrade on the cooler surface of the corona. And I also hear this unimaginable roar mingled with the tender, warm crackling of the living room logs on a cozy winter's night.

And when I hear this singing I stand dumbfounded, staggered, speechless that He is singing over me. He is rejoicing over my good with all his heart and with all his soul (see Jer. 32:41)!

A SUPERNATURAL DOORWAY CALLED EDEN

Can you imagine what the Garden must have looked like? How the angels and heavenly beings must have interacted with Adam and Eve in a cosmic dance between the two worlds? Both the supernatural realm of Glory and the natural realm were equally and harmoniously working together in one fluid motion. The Kingdom of heaven had now invaded the territory of earth and became the Kingdom of God. It was literally on *earth as it is in heaven*. The Scriptures give helpful insights into what this must have looked like, and when the dots are connected a beautiful picture of heaven on earth begins to emerge. The Bible says in Genesis 2:8:

And the Lord God planted a garden toward the east, in Eden [delight]; and there He put the man whom He had formed (framed, constituted).

It means that the Lord God planted a garden toward the east, "In Eden." It does not say that the Lord God planted the Garden of Eden, but rather that Eden was a place in the east where the Lord God planted a garden. I believe Eden was a place where the supernatural world, the Glory realm, met and was joined with the physical territory of earth. Through Eden's doorway flowed the Glory of God. Angels came through that door as well as everything Adam needed. Eden joined the two worlds in such a way that they literally became one. Not only did heaven flow through that passageway called Eden, but Adam also had access to pass from the physical realm of earth into the spirit realm. It was a two way street. Can you see the ebb and flow? How beautiful it must have been. How glorious this place called earth was. All of creation functioned at its full capacity and was fruitful in every way.

Creation listened to Adam when he spoke and obeyed his every word. The earth flourished under the loving command of Adam as God intended it to be. Adam's job was to make the physical territory of earth look like heaven in every way. There was a constant flow of heaven pouring through Eden to make this reality. The Light of the Glory of God moved through that sphere, out of the supernatural and into the natural. Genesis 2:10 tells us:

Now a river went out of Eden to water the garden; and from there it divided and became four [river] heads.

It says that there was a river that went out or flowed out of Eden and it watered the garden, and after it watered the garden, it split into four river heads and went into the earth. There was a river that flowed out of the supernatural and became a physical river that then watered the garden. Interesting! Where did this river come from? Let's look at the end of the book in Revelation 22:1-2 for the answer.

Then He showed me the river whose waters give life, sparkling like crystal, flowing out from the throne of God and of the Lamb through the middle of the broadway of the city; also, on either side of the river was the tree of life with its twelve varieties of fruit, yielding each month its fresh crop; and the leaves of the tree were for the healing and the restoration of the nations.

I find it interesting that in the beginning of the Word, in Genesis, we see a river that flows out of Eden and into the physical that waters the garden. Then, at the end of the Word, in Revelation's last chapter, after all is finished, we see this same river flowing out of the throne and of the Lamb. The Supernatural River of God that flows in Revelation is the same supernatural River that flows through Eden's door in Genesis. What does that river do? Well the first thing it did was water the Tree of Life, which Adam was commanded to eat from so he would live forever. The first instruction Adam received from the Lord God was how he was to eat. He was to eat from the Tree of Life and not from the tree of the knowledge of good and evil. We don't know how long Adam was actually living on the earth before the fall, but we can probably conclude that he had been there for a long time. Adam and Eve ate from the Tree of Life and lived! They were designed to live forever in that state of being. It says that the river was a river whose waters "give life." It was an eternal water, a life-giving water that flowed out from the throne of the Lamb. Jesus said in John 7:37 that if we would come to Him, out of our innermost being would flow rivers of living water!

This water is the Spirit of God; a Living Water that gives life. This River flowed out of heaven, through Eden's door and watered the garden that was in Eden where Adam was. Then it went into the rest of the earth. This is a healing, restorative water that brings healing to the nations. Everything this River touches causes life to spring forth.

Can you begin to see what this must have looked like? Can you hear the roar of the sound of that River as it was pouring through Eden's door? How wonderful it must have been to witness all of heaven passing through that place. Adam and Eve were fully engaged in both worlds. Adam was Earth's first Ambassador and Governor and all was in order.

ALL OF CREATION SINGS

All of creation is alive and is designed by God to praise Him. This includes the heavens, the sun, the moon, the stars and all created things; those with breath and those without, all created to Praise God.
In science we understand how stars vibrate and give off sound waves, but we can't hear them until these waves enter our atmosphere and have something denser than the vacuum of space to travel through. Creation is alive.

Praise Him, sun and moon, praise Him, all you stars of light!
Praise Him, you highest heavens and you waters above the heavens!
Let them praise the name of the Lord, for He
commanded and they were created.
He also established them forever and ever; He made a decree, which
shall not pass away [He fixed their bounds which
cannot be passed over].
Praise the Lord from the earth, you sea monsters and all deeps!
You lightning, hail, fog, and frost, you stormy wind
fulfilling His orders!
Mountains and all hills, fruitful trees and all cedars!
Beasts and all cattle, creeping things and flying birds! (Ps. 148).

Creation is alive and sings praises to God. Nature is a praise song that at times is sweet and melodious and at other times fast and furious in tempo. All of it a song of love we get to listen to and watch as it unfolds in color, sound and song. Human beings are different. If mankind will not, or cannot recognize and praise God in a season of visitation, then nature itself cannot help but cry out and release its song of praise to Him. This happened with Jesus as He was approaching Jerusalem at the Mount of Olives:

As He was approaching [the city], at the descent of the Mount of Olives, the whole crowd of the disciples began to rejoice and to praise God [extolling Him exultantly and] loudly for all the mighty miracles and works of power that they had witnessed, crying, "Blessed (celebrated with praises) is the King Who comes in the name of the Lord! Peace in heaven [freedom there from all the distresses that are experienced as the result of sin] and Glory (majesty and splendor) in the highest [heaven]!" And some of the Pharisees from the throng said to Jesus, "Teacher, reprove Your disciples!" He replied, "I tell you that if these keep silent, the very stones will cry out." (Luke 19:37-40).

Let everything that has breath and every breath of life praise the Lord! Praise the Lord! (Hallelujah!) (Ps. 150:6).

Think about it…. Stars singing. Stones crying out. Creation groaning. Everything that draws breath. It seems that everything in creation glorifies and praises God. The innate desire to praise and worship was instilled in us long before we were born. The Song of the Lord still seeks to be released through us — sometimes as a roar of love that releases power, a furious sound of spiritual warfare, a groaning of intercession, and often, a song of praise.

Through Him, therefore, let us constantly and at all times offer up to God a sacrifice of praise, which is the fruit of lips that thankfully acknowledge and confess and glorify His name. (Heb. 13:15).

ANGELS AND CREATION SING

Note also that in Revelation 5:12, that even the angels sing praises to Christ, despite the fact that they don't need a Savior (also note that their singing is not half-hearted; they sang with a loud voice). The salvation of mankind is the greatest wonder and plan of the ages. Angels sing of it even though they cannot know the depths of the plan and fully fathom its results as we do.

It was then disclosed to them that the services they were rendering were not meant for themselves and their period of time, but for you. [It is these very] things which have now already been made known plainly to you by those who preached the good news (the Gospel) to you by the [same] Holy Spirit sent from heaven. Into these things [the very] angels long to look! (1 Peter 1:12)

Still, they long to know more and for what they do know they praise the Lord Jesus Christ. 1 Peter 1:13 goes on to present what amounts to a surprise for many people: *"Every created thing"* sings praises to the Savior for His work and its results. While the entire creation was created perfect, since man's sin all creation has suffered from the results (see Rom. 8:20-21). These events recorded here underline the importance of the Scriptural teaching of creation in Genesis. The reason for this praise on the part of the entire creation is because it, too, will be delivered from the bondage of the results of our sin through the work of Christ. Without the first three chapters of Genesis these comments here make no sense, a fact that also supports the internal integrity of the Bible from beginning to end.

One might be tempted to understand the statement that the entire creation praises God in a figurative manner. But that would be a judgment made on the basis of ignorance. First of all, the entire creation praises God in that it shows forth His handiwork:

For since the creation of the world His invisible nature and attributes, that is, His eternal power and divinity, have been made intelligible and clearly discernible in and through the things that have been made (His handiworks). So [men] are without excuse (Rom. 1:20).

But, as all praise of God must be active as well as passive, we would also expect active praise of God in the creation, too. There is the song of the birds, beautiful to hear, and each bird has its own unique way to glorify its Creator in praise. Modern science has also discovered that just like the land creatures, the sea creatures, too, each have their own unique voices, some of which are very clearly musical. The eerie, yet glorious song of the whale is fascinating even for us humans to hear. And even the inanimate part of creation, even the heavens themselves, offer song as Psalm 148 reveals.

Radio astronomy has learned that the heavens are filled with stars, which are created to give off radio signals, signals which, when received by a radio, produce an incredible music, similar to the song of the whale. Even unbelieving men have noted these sounds from unexpected parts of creation. They have remarked about the amazing musical qualities of these sounds — sounds of creation itself joining with believers and angels in praise of the One who has delivered us from sin, death, and the devil!

THE REALITY OF A SINGING GOD

I want to come back to the idea of the reality of a singing God. Many scholars believe God sang the worlds into existence. If this is true, then book Hebrews 1:1-3 could have been stated something like this:

> Long ago God sang to our ancestors in many and varied songs of the Prophets, but in these last day he has sung to us by His very Song through whom He has created the ages. The song is the echo of God's Glory and the exact melody of God's very being, and God sustains all things by the Melody or Vibration of His Powerful Song...."

Again with this in mind, the beginning of the book of John would have sounded a little something like this:

> In the beginning (before all time) was the Song (Christ), and the Song was with God, and Song was God Himself. All things were made and came into existence through the Song; and without Him was not even one thing made that has come into being.

The psalms are always meant to be sung or at least recited as poetry.[2] Today the psalm proclaims:

> *Sing unto God a new song… make a joyful noise to the Lord, all the*
> *earth; break forth into joyous song and sing praises; Sing praises to*
> *the Lord with the lyre, with the sound of melody, with trumpets and*
> *the sound of the horn, make a joyful noise before the King, the Lord.*
> (Ps. 98:1-9)

ST. AUGUSTINE

St. Augustine states, "*When we sing, we are echo-ing the divine melody that still sounds throughout the cosmos. When we sing, Saint Augustine said, we pray twice.*"

God is speaking to us not just in words and reason but through the music of the heart and the universe. As we listen and sing, we become good tuning forks that resonate with the supernatural melody we hear. The angels hear this song, and as we sing we become in tune with the angelic realm and ourselves and harmonize into a proper vibration along with them. Some would say this sounds "New Age." Call it what you will. What I'm communicating to you are Kingdom truths that I have personally put into practice in my life and ministry and have seen firsthand how they manifest raw supernatural power in the realm of miracles that bring the Glory of God from the unseen realm with substance. I have received countless testimonies from people in my meetings that as we simply released a shout of praise to God, tumors would dissolve, backs were healed, ears were opened, etc. It may sound foreign to you, but these are the truths the last-days church will need to embrace in order to see heaven come with all of its fury!

And where do we hear the song? First of all, in the created world, which is the first song that God has sung; the cosmos is the music of the spheres that has been sung by God. And as God the singer has sung the song through all eternity, a song that we call the Word or Son of God, so is the Voice of Christ vibrating in the universe. Hebrews 1:2-3 says, *"Through the Son [Song]... He has also created... the ages of time... and again God sustains all things by His powerful [Song]"* (emphasis mine).

The Gospel of John 1:3 tells us that all things came into being through Him, and without Him not one thing came into being.

There is only one God. There is only one Song. Creation and Redemption are both verses of God's song. The Incarnation of Jesus Christ reinforces the song of creation, and all of many along with creation are lifted up into the Presence of the divine through the resounding song of the Living Word as He sings.

Finally, God's song comes around us and invites us to witness the secrets of both the seen and unseen realm, and attest that creation is made for truth and not denial, for praise and not self-importance. When we sing, we join with the angels announcing tidings of goods news to all the earth, and bring the reality and realm of the Glory of God and life that vibrates with supernatural life in both arenas.

String theory and vibrating energy is probably one of the most powerful supports to the theory that God sang the worlds into being— and it is my personal belief that He did.[3]

ALL SOUND MATTER IS VIBRATING ENERGY

C. S. Lewis and J. R. R. Tolkien must have thought that the idea of a Singing God was relevant. They spent time depicting this truth in their magnificent writings—*The Chronicles of Narnia* and *The Silmarillion*. The Apache and Cherokee Indians have incredibly intriguing tales of the singing creator god in their literature. In fact, folk writings from almost every culture contain such references to the idea of song as a possible—or even probable—tool used in the creation of the worlds. These ideas become viable because of their repetitions in almost every body of folk literature.

As a musician and writer, when I heard Brian Greene lecturing on public TV about "string theory", which brings these truths to light that all matter, reduced to its smallest particles, is nothing more than "vibrating strings of energy," I couldn't help but think of Jesus singing creation into being.

Taken from my book *Glory Rising*: "Jesus, as the Word, created all things. In this passage, the Greek word for "Word" is *logos*. Logos can also be interpreted into the English word "matter." So we can say: *In the beginning was the "Word," and the "Word" was with God, and the "Word" was God..."* or *"In the beginning was the "Matter," and the "Matter" was with God, and the "Matter" was God!"* (John 1:1, emphasis mine)." [4]

The spoken Word is Matter that creates substance. Therefore, we can see that words spoken in a faith-decree, come out as energized matter that materializes in the natural-realm. As we speak faith-decrees, when the Glory is thick in any place creative matter appears. Just recently I was ministering in Detroit doing five nights of a live televised Healing in America Tour. On the second night after I had preached a message on Faith that releases creative miracles, there was a man there who was born deaf in his right ear. He later testified that the doctors said he was born with his ear undeveloped and that he had none of the mechanics there for him to physically hear. Each night in the healing crusade we would release a "Shout of the Lord" that would bring the Glory of God into the room. All are encouraged to shout to the Lord for their miracles and believe for God to release miracles from His Presence.

As always, there are many that come to the front to testify of both healings and miracles that manifest from heaven. This man came forward and testified that in the "Shout" God opened his ear. He had no mechanics according to the doctors—he had never heard out of that ear—but in the Glory that night, the spoken Word was released that came out as energized matter in the room and materialized in the natural-realm and recreated this man's ear brand new! This has happened over and over around the world. I could fill the rest of the pages of this book with testimonies of accounts like this. The Word spoken in faith comes out as ENERGIZED MATTER that creates and re-creates body parts. Hallelujah!

MATTER IS A FREQUENCY SPOKEN BY JESUS

When God spoke the worlds into being all the frequencies of His Glory became manifest and the universe came into being! David Van Koevering, who helped in creating the Moog synthesizer and is a well known physics and revelatory teacher says, "...*from the tiniest vibrating superstring that is causing or SINGING the atoms into being and that make up the table of 103 elements, all the way through everything the Hubble telescope sees, are the vibrating frequencies of Jesus' voice.*" [5]

> *For by Him all things were created, both in the heavens and on earth, visible and invisible, whether thrones or dominions or rulers or authorities... He is before all things, and in Him all things hold together* (Col. 1:16-17).

The phrase *He is before all things* means that He is outside of our time. Jesus said to John the Revelator that He was and is the Alpha (beginning) and Omega (ending). Jesus is outside our concept of time in His eternal now and is causing all things to be.

SONG MATTER HAS MEMORY

When we understand by the spoken Word that we are being recreated in Christ now by His singing our song frequency, our intimacy with Him will change. His song of creation was not something He did 16 billion years ago. He is causing you to be now!

Hebrews 11:1 says that faith is substance. It is the invisible substance from which your physical world was and is being created by Jesus Christ. Annette Capps said, "God used faith substance and word energy to create the universe. He spoke and the vibration (sound) of His words released (caused) the substance that became the stars and planets."

When we understand that matter has memory and that every good or evil action, word, or thought is recorded, it is our responsibility to remove, purge, and release evil memory.

Matter has memory, and you can change everything that has been recorded by what you speak and observe, by the words you declare, or by the curses you remove and release in the name of Jesus. You can create protected places by anointing with oil and speaking blessings with your words of faith.

> *By faith we understand that the worlds were prepared by the word of God, so that what is seen was not made out of things which are visible* (Heb. 11:3).

The worlds were framed by God's Word—the seen being brought into existence from the unseen. Likewise, we can call matter from the unseen realm into the visible realm.

> *You have heard [these things foretold], now you see this fulfillment. And will you not bear witness to it? I show you specified new things from this time forth, even hidden things [kept in reserve] which you have not known. They are created now [called into being by the **prophetic word**], and not long ago; and before today you have never heard of them, lest you should say, Behold, I knew them* (Is. 48:6-7, emphasis mine).

By our spoken words, we can decree a thing, and it will come to pass!

> *You shall also decide and decree a thing, and it shall be established*

for you; and the light (of God's favor) shall shine upon your ways (Job 22:28).

MUSIC IS THE LANGUAGE OF THE SPIRIT

Dr. Jeremy Begbie, theologian, professional musician has encapsulated in one statement the essence of the quest that musicians have been on for centuries. He wrote, "It is clear that music is one of the most powerful communicative media we have, and the depth of how it communicates and what it communicates we are just beginning to understand."

PLATO

Personally, I believe music is the language of the Spirit and is understood by both the seen and unseen realm. It is a universal language that transcends boundaries and unites the heart of God with all of Creation. Angels move in the power, radiance and Light that is produced from music as it flows through the heart of mankind and every created being. Music is the language of the Spirit and has the power to not just influence the world, but to forever change it. Even the secular Greek Philosopher Plato wrote:

Music gives soul to the Universe, Wings to the Mind, Flight to the Imagination and Life to everything. - Plato

Every proton, neutron and atom is spinning with life, light and vibrating energy from the Voice of the Lord of creation. Because music is spirit language it's easy to connect the idea of a singing God. There is a great deal of support for this idea in the fields of mathematics, theology, language and science.

Much is being written and debated over the subject of Creation at this point in time, and I believe that the idea of God being a singing God figures in profoundly.

THE SINGING RIVER
MUSCLE SHOALS, ALABAMA

Most every student of Alabama history and geography learns about the State's beautiful Tennessee River, which flows generally east-to-west across North Alabama. The waters that ultimately become the Tennessee River have their headwaters in the springs and streams of the Appalachian Mountains. The area along the river in Alabama was home to several of the historical Native American tribes, each of which had their own name for the river or particular sections of it. These included the Cherokee, Chickasaw, Shawnee, Creek and Yuchi tribes.

According to Alabama historian William L. McDonald, the Cherokee Indians called the river "The Singing River" because these flowing waters sounded to them like a woman singing. In times of low water, she sang sweetly. But when the river was raging, she sounded loud and angry.

Whether it is fact or fabrication, the Legend of the Singing River is a beautiful story and description of the early Muscle Shoals. There is little doubt that in the region of Muscle Shoals, Alabama there is a sound implanted in the physical and spiritual DNA that is heavenly and purposed by God for heavens sound to be captured and released. Nashville, Tennessee has an equally popular and distinct purpose and sound and similar calling as well. There is something purposed by God for these regions that will play a part in releasing a sound for last days revival that will impact the world. The world and the secular recording industry has picked up on the sounds of these regions, but only as a shadow of what is to come!

In Muscle Shoals, a lone musician sits by the edge of the Singing River where it's flowing pace and lush, green surroundings inspire him to write a song. He is awaiting his recording session in the famous studio located behind him. Julian Lennon walks back to the Sheffield, Alabama studio and goes on to record his melodic 1984 debut album, "Valotte" that would eventually go platinum. Lennon is just one of the celebrated musicians to record in the legendary Muscle Shoals Sound Studio. Bob Dylan, The Rolling Stones, Jimmy Buffet, Bob Segar, Lynyrd Skynyrd, Paul Simon and Rod Stewart are among the numerous musicians who have all recorded albums and tracks in this venerated studio that opened in 1969 on 3614 Jackson Highway.

Muscle Shoals is known for recording many hit songs from the 1960s through today at FAME Studios, where Aretha Franklin recorded, and Muscle Shoals Sound Studio which developed work for Bob Dylan, Paul Simon and countless others. Both FAME Studios and Muscle Shoals Sound Studios are still in operation in the city. Recordings from Rod Stewart, Aretha Franklin, Eric Clapton, Lynyrd Skynyrd and The Allman Brothers, recent hit songs such as "Before He Cheats" by Carrie Underwood and "I Loved Her First" by Heartland continue the city's musical legacy. George Michael recorded an early, unreleased version of "Careless Whisper" with Jerry Wexler in Muscle Shoals in 1983.

Many Los Angeles, California recording studios have tried to copy the sound that comes from muscle shoals, yet it cannot be duplicated there because the sound arises from only one, specific region. And nature sounds cannot be cloned by digital instruments. [6]

THE BLUE STONES OF WALES

As we look at history and folklore, most people refer to the Druids as a demonized group of people bent on sorcery and witchcraft, and no doubt many were. But it is also important to understand that many of the so-called "Druids" of the day were nothing more than Welsh clans that were connected to the Lord through creation. They were a type of mystic desert people that communed with the Lord and experienced incredible revelations from the Lord of creation.

The land of Wales is known to many as the "Center of the Cosmos" because of the Blue stones of Wales that are found in the Preseli Mountains. These desert people, or Druids, moved the massive tonnage of Blue Stones from Wales to the south of England some 250 miles because of their Vibrating and healing properties. All stones vibrate, but these stones, when placed in the proper sequence and order, vibrate at another dimension creating a centrifugal harmony that is measured far beyond normal. These vibrating stones of Wales were known to bring the body, soul and spirit of an individual into alignment and not just heighten the spiritual state of an individual as they came in contact with them. They brought the body into harmony to the degree that many were healed of physical ailments and diseases — instantly! These early Welsh clans were known as early "desert fathers" that had incredible encounters with the Lord Jesus Christ as well as angelic encounters. The Roman Catholic Church branded them as a dark people because of their non-compliance with the organized church and banned them as a means to control them and dampen the effect of their pure nature. This has been the Mode of Operation of many of the dealings with the Roman Catholic Church with those that would not conform from the Jansenists, Huguenots and others as depicted in history. Granted not all were saints as in all religions, however on the same note we cannot assume that all were bad as in the case of the non-compliant Welsh and English Desert Fathers of the 13th-19th centuries.

CREATION RESPONDS TO THE VOICE OF LOVE

In every atom there is life and light. This is important to know when talking about how creation came about. When God created the universe, He breathed the galaxies out, or sang them out of His imagination. The newly created atoms were all spinning harmoniously according to their own vibration and created order; each in their own unique way. When Adam fell from the Glory of God, the result was so dramatic in the natural that it shifted the world on its axis. The atoms were literally knocked out of rhythm from their harmonious spin. Everything was affected at the sub atomic level. When this happened it opened the door for Satan to corrupt and alter things genetically. And not just genetically, but by a counter harmony… the voice of disharmony. This disharmony works against the original to bring it out of balance eventually breaking down the original that would ultimately bring forth death. But the atoms were preprogrammed to respond to the voice of love. So, if we have love emanating and harmonizing out from us, the atoms, protons, neutrons can feel us and will respond to heaven's tuning fork vibrating from us. Atoms were birthed from love and as created particles they feel love and respond to it. Animals feel it… tree's feel it… plants feel it. The atoms feel it and they will cooperate with you and form into whatever you desire in love because they recognize our sonship position as being sons and daughters of the Creator and know that we have dominion over this physical world.

What you are emanating leaves a trail and affects everything around you. It affects the physical creation, the animal creation, and every created being. If you come home with a bad attitude, without even opening your mouth, the first to tune into your attitude are your pets. Creation knows this because it is sensitized to love.

Now Paul gives us a nudge in the right direction—out of vibrating with negative emotion he promises to show us a more excellent way (see 1 Cor. 12:31), the way of love.

> *When the complete and perfect (total) comes, the incomplete and imperfect will vanish away* (1 Cor. 13:10).

When love comes we will have a more excellent and perfect way and all of creation will respond to love. Then we will have complete cooperation with creation and it will respond perfectly in the way of love. We know that creation was subjected to man and is waiting for man to walk in the way of love that will lift the curse that has been placed upon it.

> *For (even the whole) creation (all nature) waits expectantly and longs earnestly for God's sons to be made known (waits for the revealing, the disclosing of their sonship) to be made perfect in love that will change the order of things. Then... that nature (creation) itself will be set free from its bondage to decay and corruption (and gain an entrance) into the glorious freedom of (and by) God's children* (Rom. 8:19, 21).

Love is the key that creation will respond to and heaven will work with to unleash unlimited power and authority. This is the season for unprecedented miracles signs and wonders. This is the season of the love feasts of God.

Chapter 2

UNLEASHING THE FURIOUS SOUND OF HEAVEN ON EARTH

RADICAL ANOINTINGS

Several years ago I was ministering in a meeting in Plymouth, Michigan when something happened that caused me to realize the need for a consistent flow of heaven's power in my ministry. I had just finished preaching and stood up to release miracles into the room by faith decree. I always begin by thanking God for every miracle that will take place and giving Him all the Glory for everything that takes place. The Glory Presence came into the auditorium so sweet that night. People, by faith, began to claim and receive their healing and, as usual, began to come forward to testify. As people were lining up on both sides of me, I noticed an elderly, black woman get up from her front row seat and begin to approach me. I thought to myself, "Oh, Oh... here she comes... this woman is serious about something!" She yelled out at me with a loud voice:

"Man of God, my left eye is scheduled to be taken out by the doctor the day after tomorrow. He said that all the nerve endings are dead in there and that the best thing to do would be to surgically remove it and replace it with a glass eye to keep from infection. I heard about these here meetings from a friend of mine and told myself they are not going to take my eye. I was born with that eye and I'll meet Jesus with

that eye. I decided then that I was gonna go down to the meeting and get my miracle and that's the way it's going to be."

As she was speaking to me all could hear her plight. I could see that her right eye was looking directly at me and that her left eye was looking straight at the floor and unresponsive. As I approached the woman I was praying in the Spirit saying, "Lord, You need to do something… this woman won't take no for an answer!" As I reached her I said, "Then take your miracle NOW! BAM!!" and gently smacked her on the head. She crumbled to the floor in a heap, shaking under the power of God. I began to take testimonies from others who had received healing in the Presence of the Lord. A few moments later I saw the woman struggling to get to her feet. When she finally did she yelled at me again and said, "I told you I'm not leaving here until I get my miracle." As she did I noticed that both of her eyes were looking directly at me now, but she still could not see. So I ran over to her again and said, "Then take your miracle NOW!! BAM… BAM!!" and smacked her on the head again. Again she crumbled to the ground under the power of the Holy Ghost and I continued taking testimonies and thanking God for the miracle that was happening in the woman. A few moments later she was struggling to get up again, and this time when she did she let out a scream for all to hear and said, "Thank you Jesus I can see!" God had completely recreated that dead eye into a new eyeball. She danced and praised God all night long.

After seeing that sudden moment of divine intervention come and heal that woman, I remember telling the Lord that I needed an increase in power. I felt so unprepared for that kind of demand, but knew it was the beginning of a demand I would place on heaven for an increase in miracle power.

We are in a season of the release of radical new anointings that bring with it great opportunities for spiritual advancement into the supernatural. We have fully crossed over the threshold in God's timeline and the Glory of God is being revealed with fresh power and new demonstrations of the miraculous. It seems like the whole earth is groaning to see the "suddenlies" of God. Many around the world are desperate a new move of God, and the Lord promises to fill all those who hunger and thirst for Him. Those who seek the new in this season will find the new, but we must rise into these higher levels of the Glory of God. Paul and Silas were examples in the early church of what takes place when the suddenlies of God come to earth.

THE SUDDENLIES OF GOD

Paul and Silas had been unjustly arrested. Because they had cast a spirit of divination out of a girl, the local Philippian authorities beat them and then threw them into the inner dungeon deep inside the prison. However, their crisis turned into an opportunity to experience a "suddenly" of God—a moment of divine intervention that instantly changes a situation.

> *And when they had laid many stripes upon them, they cast them into prison, charging the jailor to keep them safely: Who, having received such a charge, thrust them into the inner prison, and made their feet fast in the stocks. And at midnight Paul and Silas prayed, and sang praises unto God: and the prisoners heard them"* (Acts 16:23-25).

Besides the trauma of the severe beating, they were fastened in shackles that clamped their arms and legs in an immobile position, causing cramps and loss of circulation. The atmosphere was depressing. According to the standards of that day, a prison resembled more of a dungeon; a dark, damp, stench-ridden place, with no facility for waste or comforts of any kind.

Yet, in spite of the throbbing pain in their bodies and the disheartening atmosphere, Acts 16:23-26 gives us a clue as to what these men did that ushered in the sudden intervention of heaven. At midnight Paul and Silas were heard praying and singing praises to God! What a strange sound this must have been to the other prisoners who were used to only hearing the groans or cursing of those who had been beaten. They must have been thinking, "Those stupid Christians. Where is your God now? Doesn't He have the power to save you from you situation? And what good does it do to sing?" They were about to find out that these two followers of Christ could sing their way to freedom as their praises tapped into the power of God.

> *And suddenly there was a great earthquake, so that the foundations of the prison were shaken: and immediately all the doors were opened, and everyone's bands were loosed."*

What caused this mighty discharge of power? The high praises of God vibrating through the atmosphere.

HIGH PRAISE UNLEASHES THE PRESENCE & POWER OF GOD

Paul and Silas knew how to capture the attention of heaven. They knew the power of thanksgiving and understood that High praise was the key to lifting their hearts above their situation so they could enter into God's presence and power. Not only did their shackles fall off, but everyone's shackles fell off. Their praises had the power of breakthrough to set everyone free within earshot!

Not everyone understands how to get the breakthrough, but Paul and Silas modeled it for us. In this generation there is coming a revelation and a release of the Spirit of Isaiah 61 that will result in people being set from every kind of life controlling situation and captivity.

> *The Spirit of the Lord God is upon me, because the Lord has anointed and qualified me to preach the Gospel of good tidings to the meek, the poor, and afflicted; He has sent me to bind up and heal the brokenhearted, to proclaim liberty to the [physical and spiritual] captives and the opening of the prison and of the eyes to those who are bound.* (Isa. 61:1)

Only a few know how to get the breakthrough, but when it comes, everybody's shackles fall off! God is releasing His power through a praising company that even the elements will respond to. The praise and thanksgiving of Paul and Silas reached a crescendo in the atmosphere where heaven responded with the "suddenlies" of God. The earth quaked, power was released from heaven, and all were set free.

We will see whole cities and regions overcome with this kind of atmospheric power as the saints of God release the high praises of God. The earth will respond to the resonance of the release of the Glory of God through the believers upon the earth and it will shake nations.

Psalms 22:3 says that God inhabits the praises of His people. In other words, God "dwells" or actually lives in the atmosphere of His praise. When the Praises go up, the Glory comes down. This means that praise is not merely a reaction from coming into His presence—but rather praise is a vehicle of faith that releases the presence and power of God! You release praise and it opens up heaven and brings the Glory of God down. Praise is an action exercised by faith, and when released by the believer toward God is draws heaven to earth around the individual and supernaturally changes the environment. Praise is the "gate" which allows us to enter His Glory. King David explained this principle to us when he wrote:

> *Enter into his gates with thanksgiving, and into his courts with praise:*
> *be thankful unto him, and bless his name* (Ps. 100:4).

Jesus said that His presence will inhabit the gathering of believers who congregate in His name:

> *For where two or three are gathered together in my name, there am I*
> *in the midst of them* (Matt. 18:20).

A "gathering in His name" means that Jesus must be the focus of the assembly. He must be the One preached about, sung about—the one praised and worshiped. Not only is Jesus the central focus of praise, but He stands in the midst of His brothers in the worshipping congregation and sings along with us in praise to the Father!

> *For both He Who sanctifies [making men holy] and those who are sanctified all have one [Father]. For this reason He is not ashamed to call them brethren;For He says, I will declare Your [the Father's] name to My brethren; in the midst of the [worshiping] congregation I will sing hymns of praise to You* (Heb. 2:11-13).

Think about that! Jesus calls us His brothers and when we worship the Father in Spirit and in Truth, He is standing in the middle of us singing songs of Praise—along with His brothers—to the Father. He is not ashamed to call us brothers… so we should not be ashamed to call Him brother. We both have the same Father!

A MIGHTY SHOUT IN HEAVEN

Paul and Silas understood what it took in order to get the breakthrough in their situation so that everyone in the jail benefited as well. Today there is a shift taking place in the church that will focus on Jesus Christ as the Lion of the Tribe of Judah. His roar will be heard and felt as a mighty vibration in the earth as it flows through an end-time army of God. This vibration of the Spirit will be recognized by every living thing on the earth as well as the rest of creation. Did you notice the residual effect of the praise and thanksgiving of Paul and Silas resulted in an earthquake? Creation responded with an "Amen" as these two sons of the Kingdom were harmonizing with the will of heaven! A mighty vibration, or shaking, was released from the Throne Room resulting in an earthy quaking, and creation was moved.

> *AFTER THIS I heard what sounded like a **mighty shout** of a great crowd in heaven, exclaiming, Hallelujah (praise the Lord)! Salvation and glory (splendor and majesty) and power (dominion and authori-*

*ty) [belong] to our God! And **again they shouted**, Hallelujah (praise the Lord)! **After that I heard what sounded like the shout** of a vast throng, like the **boom** of many pounding waves, and like the **roar** of terrific and mighty peals of thunder, exclaiming, Hallelujah (praise the Lord)! For now the Lord our God the Omnipotent (the All-Ruler) reigns! Let us rejoice and shout for joy [exulting and triumphant]! Let us celebrate and ascribe to Him glory and honor, for the marriage of the Lamb [at last] has come, and His bride has prepared herself* (Revelation 19:1, 3, 6-7, emphasis mine).

Revelation 19:6 refers to the "boom or sound of many pounding waves" and of "ROAR of terrific and mighty peals of thunder" as a sound of corporate worship in heaven crying "HALLELUJAH!" In this season of time the Body of Christ must learn how to synchronize earth with heaven. The best way to do this is simply do what heaven is doing on the earth. According to Revelation 19 there is a vast throng in heaven too large to be counted that releases a "Mighty Shout" and exclaims, "Hallelujah." As this is done repeatedly in heaven it reaches a peak in the Throne Room and it sounds like a "Roar."

Out from the throne came flashes of lightning and rumblings and peals of thunder, and in front of the throne seven blazing torches burned, which are the seven Spirits of God [the sevenfold Holy Spirit] (Rev. 4:5).

According to the Scriptures, it appears that the Throne Room is a violent, noisy, powerful place where flashes of lightning and rumblings are accompanied by clashes of thunder and the terrific roar of multitudes praising and shouting "Hallelujah!" Heaven is not for the faint of heart. It is a place of great dread and power! This heavenly rage is what was released when Paul and Silas synchronized heaven and earth. This power was released with such fury that every chain was broken and the earth resounded with the same quaking that was in heaven.

I'm telling you I've been in meetings around the world where the greatest of miracles that have taken place were in the High Praise of God. No man can do by the working of a gift what God will do when He releases His Glory from the Throne Room of heaven. I've seen those in wheel chairs stand up instantly, those on mats and cots in the United States and in third world countries raised up by the atmospheric power of heaven. This was the case of revival meetings we did at Great Faith Bible Church in Seoul, Korea. Six thousand people attended the nightly meetings and before we got within a city block of the church the Glory of God could be felt in the air. It was electrifying! People would show up three to four hours early just to intercede for God to move. Each night we were so drunk in the Holy Ghost we would have to be escorted (practically carried) to the pastor's office and then again, onto the stage to minister because of the overwhelming cloud of Glory that was in the atmosphere. Miracle after staggering miracle took place each night. People brought in on mats would walk out healed. Countless blind and deaf individuals were completely healed. Tumors dissolved and legs grew out all because of the atmospheric Glory of God that hovered in and around the building. It was literally like a tangible cloud you could feel.

There is not a sickness or disease known to man that can maintain its life force when the Glory of God enters the atmosphere. Sickness is instantly driven out and demons must leave in the name of Jesus Christ. The earth shakes and quakes at the Presence of the Lord. When Resurrection Life enters the room, the death causing all the peoples' emotional and physical issues, must leave.

THE KEY OF DAVID

Keys open and close doors! Just as God places them upon the "Shoulder" of the house of David, God also places them on us. David is a man who is known for his "Worship" throughout Scripture. In a sense, worship is the key to opening doors. The keys to opening doors in the realm of the Spirit were not only given to Jesus, they are available to us as well. According to Isaiah 9:6, the government of the Kingdom of God rests upon the shoulder of Jesus. For foundational purposes I want to take a quick look at the well-known Key of David Scripture passage prophesied by Isaiah. Later we will go into greater detail.

> *And the key of the house of David I will lay upon his shoulder; he shall open and no one shall shut, he shall shut and no one shall open. And I will fasten him like a peg or nail in a firm place; and he will become a throne of honor and glory to his father's house. And they will hang on him the honor and the whole weight of [responsibility for] his father's house: the offspring and issue [of the family, high and low], every small vessel, from the cups even to all the flasks and big bulging bottles (Isa. 22:22-23).*

We see this passage is not directed toward the Lord, nor does it pertain to a Messianic prophecy, but rather is directed to an individual–David which can also be directed to us:

> *And the key of the house of David I will lay upon his shoulder; he shall open and no one shall shut, he shall shut and no one shall open* (vs. 22).

The Key of the house of David is laid upon the shoulder. Keys open doors. Jesus told Peter and the church that He would give us the Keys of the Kingdom. The Bible also states that Jesus is the "Head" and we are the "Body" or the "Shoulders." When these "Keys" are laid upon the shoulder of the worshipping Body of Christ, each and every person has the potential to open doors that no one will shut, and shut doors no one will open!

BECOMING A THRONE OF HONOR AND GLORY

These worshipping, warring, Kingdom-minded overcomers will not only possess the keys of the Kingdom, but will understand how to use them. They will be able to speak into every situation, both to the natural and the supernatural realm. They will be able to open doors that no man can shut, and shut doors that no one can open. Remember, we are the only ones in creation made in His image; therefore, we have the choice to align our sound with the sound of heaven. And when this happens there will be a company of believers that will move with unlimited anointing and authority that will possess revelation knowledge of the blue prints of heaven and understand their position and point of access. This is all too exciting, but let's look at the rest of the passage:

And I will fasten him like a peg or nail in a firm place; and he will become a throne of honor and glory to his father's house (vs. 23).

Isaiah saw this company of believer and said that they would be like a peg or a nail in a firm place, like a peg that someone would use to hang a cloak or a mantle on!

...and he will become a throne of honor and glory to his father's house.

The Scripture says that, "...he will become a THRONE OF HONOR and GLORY to his father's house." Who will become a THRONE of HONOR and GLORY? The one whom the Key of the House of David rests upon. He will become unmovable to the world and will be fastened like a nail in a firm place. This individual will become a supernatural gateway for all of heaven to flow through. Even more than that, it says that *he will become a* THRONE. I'm telling you that the worshipping Son (Huious) of God in these last days will literally become the throne that the Lord Jesus Christ rests upon to reveal His Kingdom of Power and Glory! Try preaching that in some of the mainline denominational churches! None the less it is the truth! Remember, Psalms 22:3 says that God is *enthroned* upon the praises of Israel.

The throne of God literally rests on the praises of His people. What does that look like? When we begin to praise God with the understanding that He is the great King of heaven and we worship Him with this attitude and reality, the Scriptures say that His throne will literally be built upon, or come to rest on top of those praises. Wherever the High Praises of God are found on the earth is where the Throne of God will rest. Wherever the Throne of God is, the King is. Wherever the King is, there is a Kingdom. Where ever the Kingdom is, the angels are—and all of the resources of the government of that domain are present in reality as well. So when Isaiah 22:23 says, "...*and he will become a throne of honor and glory to his father's house*," that's what it literally means. We become a gateway of the Glory of God through which His Kingdom manifests.

Jesus said to Nathaniel in John 1:50-51, "...*because I said to you, I saw you beneath the fig tree, do you believe in and rely on and trust in Me? You shall see greater things than this! Then He said to him, I assure you, most solemnly I tell you all, you shall see heaven opened, and the angels of God ascending and descending upon the Son of Man!*"

When we are connected with heaven we literally become a gateway for the supernatural to manifest around us. Heaven moves up and down upon us, releasing signs, wonders, and miracles with our cooperation. God is looking for an end-time army to arise with this revelation. And I fully believe we are the generation. There is a fresh sound being released from heaven with an incredible power and Glory the world has never seen—and it's falling on individuals that will bring it to the nations of the earth. This fresh sound is the same sound that ushered in the era of the early church. It is called the Sound of a Rushing Mighty Wind.

THE SOUND OF A RUSHING MIGHTY WIND

And when the day of Pentecost had fully come, they were all assembled together in one place, When suddenly there came a sound from heaven like the rushing of a violent tempest blast, and it filled the whole house in which they were sitting. And there appeared to them tongues resembling fire, which were separated and distributed and which settled on each one of them. And they were all filled (diffused throughout their souls) with the Holy Spirit and began to speak in other (different, foreign) languages (tongues), as the Spirit kept giving them clear and loud expression [in each tongue in appropriate words] (Acts 2:1-4).

When the Holy Spirit was poured out on the early church in the upper room it came as a sound from heaven like that of a rushing mighty wind that filled the entire room. Along with that sound appeared forked tongues of flames that burned on top of everyone's heads. It was the return of the long lost government of God that was finally being restored to the earth. The ushering in of that wind and fire has changed the world and impacted every generation to date. Holy Ghost revivals and reformations throughout church history have marked the return of the government of God to planet earth along with the impacted and the influenced it has had on commoners and kings of nations. That violent release of heaven formed and forged the early church and in these last days we will see nothing less than the culminations of all those anointings poured out in a concentrated form upon an end time army of God. Heaven is violent and so will all those be who embody the true nature of the Kingdom of Heaven.

THE SOUND OF UNITY

There is a sound rising in this generation that is necessary for heaven to fully manifest on the planet. It's called the Sound of Unity. When I talk about unity, I'm not referring to everybody getting together on some kind of common ground and having unity meetings. That never works. What I'm referring to is a place where the Throne of God will literally come down upon a corporate people who have one focus alone—the Presence of Jesus. What does that look like? There was a sound released in 2 Chronicles 5 when they lifted up their voice "as one" with the trumpeters and shouted the goodness of God. There was a sound of unity in Acts 2 when the disciples were in the upper room in "one accord" in prayer and fasting waiting for the promise of the Holy Spirit by Jesus' direction. They didn't know what they were looking for exactly or how to get the promise to come, but they were in one heart and mind waiting, praying, contending, and fasting together for that promise. And when that promise came, it did as a sound of a rushing might wind, not a *rushing might wind.*

There was a sound that came in unity in Acts 4, when the Apostles were gathered together as a company of believers of "one heart and soul."

> *And now, Lord, observe their threats and grant to Your bond serv-ants [full freedom] to declare Your message fearlessly, While You stretch out Your hand to cure and to perform signs and wonders through the authority and by the power of the name of Your holy Child and Servant Jesus. And when they had prayed, the place in which they were assembled was shaken; and they were all filled with the Holy Spirit, and they continued to speak the Word of God with freedom and boldness and courage. Now the company of believ-ers was of one heart and soul, and not one of them claimed that anything which he possessed was [exclusively] his own, but eve-rything they had was in common and for the use of all. And with great strength and ability and power the apostles delivered their tes-timony to the resurrection of the Lord Jesus, and great grace (lov-ing-kindness and favor and goodwill) rested richly upon them all.* (Acts 4:29-33, emphasis mine)

They were *one heart and soul* waiting for a second empowering of the Holy Ghost which came and filled them with great *boldness and courage* to preach. And the sound that came from heaven was like that of a great earthquake that shook the place they were gathered. This generation is go-ing to see the same union of shaking as God releases the violence of heaven upon a unified corporate body. We again will testify to the resurrection of the Lord Jesus Christ and GREAT GRACE will rest richly on all of us.

THE SOUND OF BREAKER ANOINTING

We're in a season in which we will again witness firsthand the sound of the armies of heaven being released in America and the nations of the earth in the Spirit of Revival. I've been privileged to minister in crusades, revivals and meetings around the world in which the power from heaven manifests and results in amazing demonstrations of miraculous power. I've watched as the angelic army of heaven descends on the masses in Africa resulting in mass deliverance of demonic strongholds. Cripples walk, blind people are healed, tumors dissolve, deaf ears open, and children walk for the first time along with countless other demonstrations of raw supernatural power. Heaven responds to the initiatives of the saints on the earth.

A while back while doing a crusade in Indonesia I witnessed the breaker anointing for miracles sweep through the stadium. I barely finished preaching when people began to cry out as fire from heaven and a breaker anointing was poured out upon them. Many began to get out of wheelchairs, throw down their crutches and run. Tumors evaporated and screams could be heard throughout the arena. God was releasing Breakthrough Anointing in a drastic way that no one in the arena could deny. The place was electrified with shouting and praise.

JESUS THE MASTER OF BREAKTHROUGH

God's plan for the earth and for us did not change after the fall. Immediately He set His plan in motion to restore the Kingdom to us and sent Jesus to get it all back for us. Jesus Christ is the ultimate Master of breakthrough who has broken open the heavens for us—so we could not only receive the Kingdom of power and authority by the Holy Spirit here on the earth—but also so we would have access to the heavenly realm with Him.

*Therefore, brethren, since we have full freedom and confidence to en-
ter into the [Holy of] Holies [by the power and virtue] in the blood
of Jesus, By this fresh (new) and living way which He initiated and
dedicated and opened for us through the separating curtain (veil of
the Holy of Holies), that is, through His flesh* (Heb. 10:19-20)

Jesus broke open the way back into the Holy place. Micah calls him the
(Messiah) ultimate Breaker;

*The Breaker [the Messiah] will go up before them. They will break
through, pass in through the gate and go out through it, and their
King will pass on before them, the Lord at their head* (Mic. 2:13).

As King David was waiting for direction from the Lord to move against the
Philistines, he was told to wait for the sound:

*When David inquired of the Lord, He said, You shall not go up, but
go around behind them and come upon them over opposite the mulberry (or balsam) trees. And when you hear the sound of marching in
the tops of the mulberry trees, then bestir yourselves, for then has the
Lord gone out before you to smite the army of the Philistines. And
David did as the Lord had commanded him, and smote the Philistines from Geba to Gezer* (2 Sam. 5:23-25).

King David knew that his only hope would be in the complete and udder
dependence upon the armies of heaven to accomplish the impossible. David had just recaptured the Ark of the Covenant that was taken by the Philistines and was in the process of bringing it back to the city of David. But
in order for this to happen he had to deal one last time with the enemies of
Israel. David's trust was in the God of the Breakthrough:

*David inquired of the Lord, saying, Shall I go up against the Philis-
tines? Will You deliver them into my hand? And the Lord said to David, Go up, for I will surely deliver [them] into your hand. And David*

*came to "**Baal-perazim**," and he smote them there, and said, The Lord has broken through my enemies before me, like the bursting out of great waters. So he called the name of that place "**Baal-perazim**" [**Lord of breaking through**].There the Philistines left their images, and David and his men took them away* (2 Sam. 5:19-20, emphasis mine).

David inquired of the Lord and God gave him heaven's strategy. Even though in this text the angels are not directly mentioned, it was the assistance of the armies of heaven that brought about the breakthrough David needed. The victory was such a massive blow to the Philistines that they didn't even have time to collect their images but just left them behind for David and his men to destroy! David called the place "*Baal-perazim*" which means, "*God of the Breakthrough.*" This massive breakthrough was manifest by the release of the Sound of angels marching on the tops of the Mulberry trees. By the way, Mulberry trees are also known as the "balm" trees, or the "healing" trees. The angels and healing go together.

I believe we are going to see in this season whole cities, regions and even nations overrun by the power of heaven evidenced by a release of the Sound of Heaven on earth. Angelic armies will descend with a sound of fire and wind that will unleash the Spirit of Revival over cites that will literally change culture as we know it. The multitudes will come to the Brightness of our Rising (see Isaiah 60, AMP) and spiritual hunger will be the catalyst for these *suddenlies* of God. The Lord will literally release the "roar" of His voice over a region; the earth will shake as all of heaven breaks loose!

*The Lord will thunder and **roar** from Zion and **utter His voice** from Jerusalem, and the heavens and the earth shall shake; but the Lord will be a refuge for His people and a stronghold to the children of Israel* (Joel 3:16, emphasis mine).

*The Lord roars out of Zion and **utters His voice** from Jerusalem* (Amos 1:2, emphasis mine).

THE VOICE OF THE LORD IS CREATIVE POWER

Several years ago on Good Friday, we were preparing to close down the Global Fire offices for the holiday weekend when my wife Jan frantically came busting into the office. She informed me that she was on the way to the grocery store with her mother and my then four-year-old daughter Mercy Rain when they spotted a tornado on the ground which was coming directly for the office. Without thinking I told my cameraman, Rayne Warne, to grab a video camera along with my personal assistant, Eric Green, to follow me outside. As we stood in front of the office it was obvious to all of us that this was no small tornado—it was in full F-4 power on the ground and was moving toward us. Without thinking I told Rayne to start filming and said, "Hey guys, watch this... In the name of Jesus Christ of Nazareth I command you, tornado, do not touch my house and dissipate, in the name of Jesus Christ." All were in amazement as the F-4 tornado instantly dissolved and lifted up over the top of us. We found out later that it did set down on the other side of the city and do some damage. Meanwhile, God demonstrated the power of the spoken word. The Voice of the Lord is in us and is a Creative Power!

LOGOS MATTER

"In the beginning was the Word, and the Word was with God, and the Word was God" (John 1:1). As stated earlier, Jesus, as the Word, created all things. In this passage, the Greek word for "Word" is *logos*. Logos can also be interpreted into the English word "matter." So we can say: *In the beginning was the "Matter", and the "Matter" was with God, and the "Matter" was God!*

The spoken Word is Matter that creates substance. Therefore, we can see that words spoken in a faith-decree, come out as energized matter that materialize in the natural-realm. As we speak faith-decrees, when the Glory is thick in an atmosphere, spontaneously, creative matter appears from the unseen realm.

For by Him all things were created, both in the heavens and on earth, visible and invisible, whether thrones or dominions or rulers or authorities... He is before all things, and in Him all things hold together (Col. 1:16-17).

The phrase *"He is before all things"* means that He is outside of our time. Jesus said to John the Revelator that He was and is the Alpha (beginning) and Omega (ending). Jesus is outside our concept of time and is eternal now, causing all things to be.

Matter and the Spirit realm are intimately connected. As it was in the beginning during Creation, so it is now. The Voice of the Lord is creative Power. There is a non-physical reality that we need to acknowledge before we can see the reality of the supernatural. Beyond the physical, we are immersed in the spiritual realm that causes matter to exist. Let's look at Psalm 29:

Ascribe to the Lord, O sons of the mighty, ascribe to the Lord glory and strength. Give to the Lord the glory due to His name; worship the Lord in the beauty of holiness or in holy array. **The voice of the Lord** *is upon the waters; the God of glory thunders; the Lord is upon many (great) waters.* **The voice of the Lord** *is powerful;* **the voice of the Lord** *is full of majesty.* **The voice of the Lord** *breaks the cedars; yes, the Lord breaks in pieces the cedars of Lebanon. He makes them also to skip like a calf; Lebanon and Sirion (Mount Hermon) like a young, wild ox.* **The voice of the Lord** *splits and flashes forth forked lightning.* **The voice of the Lord** *makes the wilderness tremble; the Lord shakes the Wilderness of Kadesh.* **The voice of the Lord** *makes the hinds bring forth their young, and His voice strips bare the forests, while in His temple everyone is saying, Glory! The Lord sat as King over the deluge; the Lord [still] sits as King [and] forever!*
The Lord will give [unyielding and impenetrable] strength to His people; the Lord will bless His people with peace (Ps. 29, emphasis mine).

Seven times in eleven verses a statement is made about the Voice of the Lord. The first is "The Voice of the Lord is upon the waters…." This is the Genesis creation account:

> *The earth was without form and an empty waste, and darkness was upon the face of the very great deep. The Spirit of God was moving (hovering, brooding) over the face of the waters. And God said, Let there be light; and there was light* (Gen. 1:2-3).

The Spirit of God was moving over the face of the waters and the Voice of the Lord said, "Let there be light" and there was light.

Psalm 29 says the Voice of the Lord is Powerful, Full of Majesty, breaks the cedars, makes the wilderness tremble and shakes the Wilderness. The Voice of the Lord flashes forth forked lightning, and makes the hinds bring for their young. The Voice of the Lord strips bare the forests while in His temple everyone is saying, GLORY!

YOU ARE A SONG

Your body was created by the voice of the Lord, calling mankind to be and it is sustained by Jesus holding all things together by *The Mighty Word of His Power* (see Heb. 1:3). David Van Koevering states in his book Physics of the Supernatural Realm, "He is singing your song. That's right! You're a song. Molecular biologists convert protein sequences into classical music. You are a song. You can send these guys a swab of your DNA, put it in a plastic bag, and they will send you back the melodies, Literally! My faith says that I'm a song sung by Jesus Christ causing me to be 20,000 times a nanosecond." [7]

THE POWER OF CREATIVE SPEAKING

The Voice of the Lord is creative power. Everything God created, He created through the power of speaking words. The Voice of the Lord is a vibration that shakes and recreates the wilderness. It has the power to both create and recreate. When God speaks we become impregnated with His word or matter. As time passes, that word grows and develops—eventually causing us to give birth to those specific promises. However, when God's word is spoken in the realm of Glory, the time it takes for the word to grow and mature is reduced to only a few moments as time is made to serve those who know and understand their rights as citizens of heaven. When we experience the Glory of God we are experiencing the realm of timelessness. Just as the Voice of the Lord has creative power, so does the voice of the sons of the Kingdom. As born again, Spirit filled believers, we are made in His image, and like God, hold the same position and place to speak with the voice of creative authority as He does. This may seem to be a stretch for some but nonetheless is altogether true.

When we are born again, we receive with the Spirit of God all the DNA and genetics that are in Him. The God who created the seen and unseen worlds dwells inside of us—this is a mystery and a beauty. The Godhead, the fullness of Deity, makes His home inside our hearts. Paul says that we should not behave as mere men (see 1 Cor. 3:3). This is because we are far from being mere men—we are possessed by Creator God.

Think about another statement of Paul's:

> ...*the Spirit of Him who raised Jesus from the dead dwells in you* (Rom. 8:11).

What type of human being does this really make you? It makes us like God in the earth. Not that we are God, but we are sons of God and made in His Image. We are "Godlike ones." The Lord told Moses:

See, I make you as God to Pharaoh (Ex. 7:1).

We literally speak as "Oracles" or as God's earthly representatives on the planet! By releasing the Voice of the Lord through the power of the Spoken Word, we can decree a thing and it will come to pass. It will happen! And it's all done by speaking words of faith.

> *You shall also decide and decree a thing, and it shall be established for you; and the light [of God's favor] shall shine upon your ways* (Job 22:28).

There are both physical and spiritual requirements for releasing the miraculous. We need the cloud of the Glory of God's Presence, and then we must understand how to speak into it. It's time for us to switch gears and start speaking Glory Presence Decrees in order to operate in the higher realities of Creative Miracles.

Chapter 3

WE SPEAK AS THE ORACLES OF GOD
THE SOUND OF REVIVAL PAST & PRESENT

GET READY FOR THE SOUND OF THE NEW WONDER-WORKING ORACLES OF GOD

We need to get ready for the new wonder workers! These new Oracles of God will change cities, regions and nations as they speak as the voice of God in the earth with the Mighty Word of power! They will move with unlimited anointing of Sound and Light that comes from the Presence of the Lord. Nothing will stand before them. To date we have seen many waves of revival hit the nations of the earth and the shores of America, but nothing like we are beginning to witness now. God has propelled the maturing Body of Christ into a new place on the planet. Miracles and power evangelism is becoming common on the streets of America and the world. A company of New Oracles is rising up with the burning coals of heaven on their lips. Like Moses, they will speak as small "g" "gods," little "Elohim" creators in the earth, as "God-like ones" declaring and decreeing the very will of God through their word.

The multitudes will understand who God is as hundreds, thousands, and even millions come to Christ through demonstrations of these new wonder-working Oracles of power. We've seen some pretty remarkable things in past revivals including the Welsh revival, The Great Awakening, Azusa Street, Latter Rain, The Voice of Healing of the 1940s and 1950s and then later moves of God like the Toronto Blessing, Brownsville Revival and even the much scrutinized Lakeland Revival. Impressive as they were, they have all been merely "previews of the coming attraction." They will all pale in comparison to the outpouring of this new season—the Outpouring of the Spirit of Revival.

The church is growing into the revelation that we really are God's representatives on this planet. And as His Governmental representatives on the earth we have been given the authority, ability and position to function with full legal Kingdom rights to administer the job. I can think of many events during my years of ministry, where as I came into a region and the Holy Spirit gave me something specific to say that would release a sign to all that were listening. God would back up the words He gave me with incredible signs in the natural. One such event was in 2006, on the 100-year anniversary of the Azusa street revival. I was ministering in Topeka, Kansas with a friend of mine and I began to prophesy in the conference center a specific word of the Lord. And to confirm that this really was a "Word from the Lord" I said that it would be backed up in the natural by ninety-mile per hour straight-line winds that would blow through the city and hail would fall from the heavens. Now this was the end of March and Spring was in the air. That evening, the weather changed. And on March 13, 2006 the front page of the *Topeka Capital Journal* read, "*Hail in Topeka reached size of golf balls and Straight-line winds reached up to ninety miles per hour.*"

WE SPEAK AS THE ORACLES OF GOD

We are in a fresh season of outpouring globally. God is unleashing something fresh from the Presence of the Lord that will result in churches, cities and regions ignited in revival fire like we've never seen before. Attesting signs and wonders will follow the anointed preaching of the Rhema Word that flows from men and women of God. We are God's mouthpieces on the planet. Peter said:

> Whoever speaks, [let him do it as one who utters] oracles of God; whoever renders service, [let him do it] as with the strength which God furnishes abundantly, so that in all things God may be glorified through Jesus Christ (the Messiah). To Him be the glory and dominion forever and ever (through endless ages). Amen (so be it) (1 Peter 4:11, emphasis mine).

Oracle preaching, or Rhema preaching, under the anointing is and always has been, the standard for every generation. We literally speak as "Oracles" or as God's representatives on the planet! His words are our words. By releasing the Voice of the Lord through the power of the Spoken Word, we can decree a thing and it will come to pass. It will happen! People do not talk about oracles very much. To many, *oracle* is a "religious" word, one used by those interested in religion. However "oracle" occurs 21 times in Scripture and it carries an important meaning. What is an oracle? Are they people who let demons speak through them... or does the Spirit of God, the Holy Spirit, speak through a them? Can anyone be an oracle?

Webster's Second International Dictionary defines an oracle as, "The conduit by which God reveals hidden knowledge or makes known His divine purpose."

One may recognize common words to the word *oracle* such as "oration," "orator," "oratory" and "orison." They all find their root in the Latin verb *orare*: to pray, utter or speak.

So an oracle is a *conduit of a message*. It is not a "medium" as in New Age spiritists who channel demonic entities. The term here, means the package the message comes through — much like a television is a conduit of movies and news, or a pastor is a conduit of the heart of God.

The most famous oracle in classical antiquity illustrates this medium-message connection. In central Greece, at the foot of Mount Parnassus, lies the town of Putho, wherein lived the Delphian oracle, a priestess who chanted prophetic messages—oracles. Those seeking to know their future flocked to her. In Greek mythology, a serpent, Puthon, inspired and guarded the priestess, that is, the oracle. The god Apollo killed the dragon and, appropriating his name, called himself Pythius. He named the priestess/oracle the Pythia.

So, the person who voiced the revelation of Puthon (and later of Apollo) was the Delphian oracle, or the Pythia. But the gods' revelations themselves were also oracles.

Surprisingly, Puthon is even mentioned once in the Bible. Paul, Luke and Timothy had not been too long in Philippi when they ran into a certain damsel possessed with a spirit of divination (see Acts 16:16). The word "divination" is *puthon* in Greek, the source of our English word *python*. Demons are the source of pagan worship (see 1 Cor. 10:20). The young lady, probably not herself the Pythia, was possessed by a spirit of divination that spoke as a demonic voice or a dark oracle to reveal information to individuals for money. In all likelihood, that demon's name is Apollo, perhaps an associate of the Apollyon of Revelation 9:11. [8]

LOGOS – WORD – ORACLE

It is not at all surprising that the Greek word translated as *oracle* in the King James Version of the New Testament is driven from *"logos"* or *"word."* That Greek word is *"logion,"* a diminutive of *logos*. *Vine's Expository Dictionary of New Testament Words* defines *logion* as "a divine response or utterance, an oracle." You may be asking yourself why all the fuss over this word Oracle. Well, it's not so much about the word as the revelation and application behind it. We are God's Ambassadors, according to 2 Corinthians 15:20. And as Ambassadors, we are to speak as God's anointed representatives on the earth, declaring His will by direct revelation, or divine "hook up" through the administration of the Holy Spirit of God. We are to speak as His divinely inspired prophets and priests, representing the will of the King. Revelation 5:9 and Exodus 19 states that He calls us to be a Kingdom of Priests on the earth. Great men in the Old and New Testaments were called "oracles" including Moses and Stephen.

Moses received the *living oracles*—specific utterances from God to give to us! Moses met with God on Mount Sinai in Exodus 3 and received direct instructions to speak to the children of Israel and to Pharaoh concerning the release of the Hebrews. The Lord told Moses: *"See, I make you as God to Pharaoh"* (Ex. 7:1).

MOSES

Moses both acted with powerful signs and wonders and spoke as a *living Oracle*—a direct messenger of God as he released the Word of the Lord to Pharaoh and backed it up with the ten plagues on Egypt. Moses was the friend of God. God spoke with Moses not like he did with any other man but He spoke with Moses *face to face.*

And the Lord spoke to Moses face to face, as a man speaks to his friend. Moses returned to the camp, but his minister Joshua son of Nun, a young man, did not depart from the [temporary prayer] tent (Ex. 33:11, emphasis mine).

King David received revelation from the Presence of the Lord and as a preface to his last words tells us that, *"The Spirit of the Lord spoke by me, and His word was on my tongue. The God of Israel said,*

KING DAVID

the Rock of Israel spoke to me" (2 Sam. 23:2).

The Prophet Jeremiah had a similar experience later. *"Then the Lord put forth His hand and touched my mouth, and the Lord said to me: 'Behold, I have put My words in your mouth'"* (Jer. 1:9). Take a look also at Jeremiah 36:2, where God commands Jeremiah to write down *"all the words that I have spoken to you against Israel, against Judah, and against all the nations."*

JEREMIAH

The message of the apostles came from God. They did not speak myths. Those people lacking the ears to hear His revelation will turn quickly enough to the Pythia who speaks under inspiration of the serpent Python and the demon Apollo.

THE STONING OF STEPHEN THE MARTYR

In Acts 7, we see Stephen on trial about to be stoned for the testimony of Jesus. He spoke of Moses being God's representative mouthpiece from the Mountain to the children of Israel.

Acts 7:38 says, *"This is he who was in the congregation in the wilderness with the Angel who spoke to him in Mount Sinai, and with our fathers, the one who received the **living oracles** to give to us"* (emphasis mine).

We understand that all Scripture is given to us by inspiration of the Holy Spirit and comes to us as living utterances or Oracles from God. This can best be described in the words of the Apostle Paul who penned most of the New Testament under direct influence of, and by direct revelation of, the

Lord Jesus Christ. Look at what Paul states:

> For I want you to know, brethren, that the Gospel which was pro-
> claimed and made known by me is not man's gospel [a human in-
> vention, according to or patterned after any human standard]. For
> indeed I did not receive it from man, nor was I taught it, but [it came
> to me] through a [direct] revelation [given] by Jesus Christ (the Mes-
> siah). Nor did I [even] go up to Jerusalem to those who were apostles
> (special messengers of Christ) before I was, but I went away and re-
> tired into Arabia, and afterward I came back again to Damascus.
> (Gal. 1:11-12, 17).

PAUL RECEIVES THE GOSPEL BY DIRECT REVELATION OF THE HOLY GHOST

> What advantage then has the Jew or what is the profit of circumci-
> sion? Much in every way! Chiefly because to them were committed
> the oracles of God (Rom. 3:1-2).

Paul extends the meaning of *oracles* here in two ways—in content and
audience:

> The word [logos] which God sent to the children of Israel, preaching
> peace by Jesus Christ—He is Lord of all—that word you know, which
> was proclaimed throughout all Judea, and began from Galilee after
> the baptism which John [the Baptist] preached (Acts 10:36-37).

Peter came to recognize that the oracles of God are for all men, God showing no partiality or favoritism (see Acts 10:34).

> For though by this time you ought to be teachers, you have need
> again for someone to teach you the elementary principles of the ora-
> cles of God, and you have come to need milk and not solid food
> (Heb. 5:12, NASB).

In context, God tells us one of the purposes of His revelation to mankind. The writer of Hebrews scolds his audience for being *dull of hearing* (vs. 11). Using an analogy of milk, the nourishment of children, against *strong meat* (vs. 12, KJV), the fare of those *who are of full age*, he laments that he needs to go back to the basics, the first principles of God's revelation. Not using that revelation to *exercise their senses to discern both good and evil* (vs. 14). They had failed to grow up!

The purpose of God's revelation is to provide the nourishment, the food, by which we come *to a perfect man, to the measure of the stature of the fullness of Christ* (see Eph. 4:13). It is God's revelation, His oracles, which allow us to go on to perfection (see Heb. 6:1).

Aside from this, Webster's definition seems to fit the biblical use of the word *oracle*. God's Word makes it clear that His oracles are His *utterances*, His revelation to mankind. Also, God uses *people* to communicate His message. The Logos Himself, as well as Moses, all the prophets and the apostles, served as oracles of God. *"If anyone speaks, let him speak as the oracles of God"* (1 Peter 4:11).

JESUS

Jesus Christ speaks as an Oracle from the Father – *Christ only spoke the words He heard His Father Speak.* Of course He is the greatest example in all Scripture of One who spoke only was directed by God. He is the Word of God in human flesh — the One by whom the worlds have their existence. The Hebrew writer says it like this:

IN MANY separate revelations each of which set forth a portion of the Truth] and in different ways God spoke of old to [our] forefathers in and by the prophets, [But] in the last of these days He has spoken to us in [the person of a] Son, Whom He appointed Heir and lawful Owner of all things, also by and through Whom He created the worlds and the reaches of space and the ages of time [He made, produced, built, operated, and arranged them in order].3He is the sole expression of the glory of God [the Light-being, the out-raying or radiance of the divine], and He is the perfect imprint and very image of [God's] nature, upholding and maintaining and guiding and propelling the universe by His mighty word of power. When He had by offering Himself accomplished our cleansing of sins and riddance of guilt, He sat down at the right hand of the divine Majesty on high (Heb. 2:1-3).

In the Gospel of John, Christ Jesus Himself attests to this more than once:

I have many things to say and to judge concerning you: but He who sent Me is true; and I speak to the world those things which I heard from Him (John 8:26).

For I have not spoken on My own authority; but the Father who sent Me gave Me a command, what I should say and what I should speak (John 12:49).

The words that I speak to you I do not speak on My own authority; but the Father who dwells in Me does the works (John 14:10).

The word which you hear is not Mine but the Father's who sent Me (John 14:24).

For I have given to [the disciples] the words which You have given Me, and they have received them… (John 17:8).

By example, Jesus walked, listened to and lived continually in unbroken fellowship with the Father and the Holy Spirit. He roll modeled the standard for all Spirit filled believers, assuring us that He would never leave us as orphans but would come to us and make His home in us.

Jesus answered, If a person [really] loves Me, he will keep My word [obey My teaching]; and My Father will love him, and We will come to him and make Our home (abode, special dwelling place) with him (John 14:23).

By this promise and outpouring of the Holy Spirit of God we are able to walk in unbroken fellowship in the Presence of God and speak as living oracles of the Kingdom of God everywhere we go. The world is looking for the real Jesus Christ. He really is the desire of the nations; they just don't know it, because they haven't really seen Him. The church has not properly revealed Jesus Christ in the way He would be seen, but this is about to change!

God is raising up an end time warrior bride that will be moved by the impulses of His heart. They will only speak what they hear the Father speaking. When this happens, such power and authority will be released from heaven that the world will recognize and respond to Him, and this is what is being worked in and through the church of Jesus Christ now. God is preparing the church to display power and Glory like the world has never seen before. Jesus Christ will be glorified in and through His church in these last days and will reap the reward of His suffering!

ORACLES OF PAST REVIVAL

It's important to understand that there were Oracles of God speaking in both the New and Old Testament, and that all of the revivals to date were initiated by men and women that moved and spoke under divine inspiration and revelation as living oracles. We are to follow the same lead in this season. Not all preaching was divinely inspired, however, wherever there is a true move of God in the earth you can rest assured that God was there speaking and moving through people that were completely yielded to Him. This is the case with such recent revivalist that most of us have either heard of or a familiar with.

CHARLES FINNEY

CHARLES FINNEY (born 1792) used to hold individuals and crowds under the power of his every word speaking as an authoritative Oracle of God:

"I received overwhelming baptisms of the Holy Ghost, that went through me, as it seemed to me, body and soul. I immediately found myself endued with such power from on high that a few words dropped here and there to individuals were the means of their immediate conversion. My words seemed to fasten like barbed arrows in the souls of men. They cut like a sword. They broke the heart like a hammer. Multitudes can attest to this. Oftentimes a word dropped without me remembering it, would fasten conviction."

Finney explains how he would sometimes lose this incredible oracle anointing and what he did to come back under it again:

"Sometimes I would find myself, in a great measure, empty of this power. I would go out and visit, and find that I made no saving impression. I would exhort and pray, with the same result. I would then set apart a day for private fasting and prayer, fearing that this power departed from me, and would inquire anxiously after the reason of this apparent emptiness. After humbling myself and crying out for help, the power would return upon me with all its freshness. This has been the experience of my life."

He continues:

"This power is a great marvel. I have many times seen people unable to endure the word. The most simple and ordinary statement would cut men off from their seats like a sword, would take away their bodily strength and render them almost as helpless as dead men. Several

times it has been true in my experience that I could not raise my voice, or say anything in prayer or exhortation except in the mildest manner, without wholly overcoming those who were present. This was not because I was preaching terror to the people; but the sweetest sounds of the gospel would overcome them. This power seems sometimes to pervade the atmosphere of one who is highly charged with it. Many times great numbers of persons in a community will be clothed with this power, when the very atmosphere of the whole place seems to be charged with the life of God. Strangers coming into it and passing through the place will be instantly smitten with conviction of sin, and in many instances converted to Christ."

"When Christians humble themselves and consecrate their all afresh to Christ, and ask for this power, they will often receive such a baptism that they will be instrumental in converting more souls in one day than in all their lifetime before. When Christians remain humble enough to retain this power the work of conversion will go on, till whole communities and regions of country are converted to Christ." [9]

GEORGE WHITEFIELD

Of this event an eyewitness writes:

"...with the sight of thousands and thousands, some in coaches, some on horseback, and some in the trees, and at times all affected and drenched in tears together, to which sometimes was added the solemnity of the approaching evening was almost too much for, and quite overcame me."[10]

GEORGE WHITEFIELD

George was surprised how crowds "...so scattered abroad can be gathered at so short a warning." He was also surprised at how such enormous crowds could listen to attentively that as he wrote, "Even in London, I never observed so profound a silence."

Benjamin Franklin heard Whitfield preach when he first arrived in Philadelphia, and wrote in response, "He had a loud and clear voice, and articulated his words and sentences so perfectly, that he might be heard and understood at a great distance, especially as his auditories, however numerous observed the most exact silence." Franklin calculated that Whitfield's voice could be heard by more than thirty thousand listeners.[11]

JOHNATHAN
EDWARDS

JOHNATHAN EDWARDS

This was more than natural ability—it was a voice of supernatural power. Sarah Edwards hosted George in Northampton, Massachusetts and wrote:

"It is wonderful to see what a 'spell' he casts over an audience by proclaiming the simple truths of the Bible. I have seen upwards of a thousand people hung on his words with breathless silence, broken only by an occasional half suppressed sob...."[12]

MARIA
WOODWORTH-ETTER

MARIA WOODWORTH-ETTER

Maria Woodworth-Etter often spoke to the crowds with such anointing that the Holy Spirit overcame the listeners and they succumbed to a trance like state. Her words were so weighty from heaven that even the toughest of individuals could not withstand the power of the Spirit by whom she spoke. Maria Woodworth-Etter responded to God's call and people were thronging to hear her speak with signs and wonders following. By 1885, without a public address system, crowds of over twenty-five thousand pressed in to hear her minister while hundreds fell to the ground under the power of God. Those who came to investigate, condemn, or harass her seemed most at risk of "falling out" in what was described as a trance-like state. Woodworth-Etter not only shook up denominational religion, she rocked the secular world with life-altering displays of God's power. [13]

ORACLE PREACHING

Maria Woodworth-Etter demonstrated "Oracle" preaching and stated, "These strong manifestations of the Spirit were nothing new; they were just something the Church had lost." She was unwavering in her determination to break the strongholds that held people, communities, and whole cities in bondage. It seemed like the more opposition she faced, the more she dug in her heels. Maria produced invincible strength through tenacious prayer that enabled her to take authority and minister with grace and power. She was known as a revivalist who could break towns open. Earlier in her ministry, Maria received a vision from the Lord where she saw people bundled up like sheaves of wheat lying in a field. It was not until she preached with power at a church in western Ohio that the meaning of her vision about the sheaves of wheat became clear. Here the people fell into what seemed like "trances"—an altered state which would come to profoundly mark her ministry and confound the wise of her day. "Fifteen came to the altar screaming for mercy. Men and women fell and lay like dead," Maria recounted. "After laying on the floor for some time, they sprang to their feet shouting praises to God. The ministers and elder saints wept and praised the Lord for His 'Pentecost Power'"—and from that meeting on, her ministry would be marked by this particular manifestation with hundreds miraculously healed, and hundreds more coming to Christ.

At every meeting she held, there was a demonstration of the power of the Spirit. One reporter wrote, "Vehicles of all sorts began pouring into the city at an early hour—nothing short of a circus or a political rally ever before brought in so large a crowd." Maria couldn't answer all the invitations she received to minister, but the ones she did accept created a national stir that has never been silenced. The writings of then young F.F. Bosworth described the spectacular meetings that took place in Dallas, Texas, from July through December. As a result, Dallas became a hub of the Pentecostal revival.

She has been called the grandmother of the Pentecostal movement. None has done more than Maria Woodworth-Etter to shed light on the convicting power of the Holy Spirit, the role of women in ministry, and the power of miracle crusades to revive a nation. In addition, she brought insight on how to effectively administrate massive miracle crusades, build sustainable ministry centers and manage opposition in the public arena. Her commitment and dedication personally influenced such great heroes of the faith as Smith Wigglesworth, Aimee Semple McPherson, John Alexander Dowie, John G. Lake, E.W. Kenyon, F.F. Bosworth, and Kathryn Kuhlman.

Her legacy is evidenced by the ongoing ministry work of healing evangelists around the world. Though, for the last six years of her life, she confined herself to ministering from the Tabernacle she had erected in Indianapolis, Indiana, her healing anointing remained as powerful as ever. She continued to speak with power from the Word of God until her very last days. As she became weaker, she was carried in a chair to the pulpit, and finally ministered a touch of healing or a word of hope from her bed.[14]

WILLIAM BRANHAM - AN ORACLE OF GOD IN THE '50'S HEALING REVIVAL

William Branham was beyond doubt a man of notable signs and wonders. From birth, supernatural manifestations marked his life. He truly walked with God. He did indeed have a divine impartation to minister healing and deliverance. A modern day prophet of biblical proportion, he healed the multitudes and delivered the afflicted from all kinds of demonic bondages

WILLIAM BRANHAM

and strongholds. He walked in the Spirit, guided by visions from the angel of the Lord and when he spoke to individuals or the masses, he spoke as God's mouthpiece. He truly spoke as an Oracle of God in the healing revival. Many of the known healing evangelists came alongside him to promote and partner with him—men such as Gordon Lindsey, A.A. Allen, F.F. Bosworth, and Jack Moore. Branham's healing team launched what became known as the Voice of Healing magazine, which helped fuel the great healing revival of the early 1950s. This movement directly impacted T.L. Osborn, Kenneth Hagin, Oral Roberts, and others so that today the wider church has a firmer grasp on the truths regarding faith and healing.

MEAGER BEGINNINGS

William Marrion Branham was born to a fifteen-year-old mother, and an eighteen-year-old father, in a tiny, dirt floor shack up in the hills of Kentucky. They were poor and illiterate, and had no interest in spiritual matters. William grew up without any knowledge of God, the Bible, or prayer. Yet God had a special call on his life and would go to great lengths throughout William's childhood to get his attention. From a young age, William heard God's voice, and knew that he was being called to a different kind of life than those around him.

He didn't understand the calling or how to quiet the longing he felt in his heart. At the age of nineteen he decided to move away hoping that he would find solace in a new location. He moved to Phoenix, Arizona where he worked on a ranch, but he still couldn't escape the sense that God was calling him. When he received news that his brother had died, he returned home to his grief-stricken family. It was at the funeral that he heard his first prayer and knew then that he needed to learn to pray.

ANSWERING THE CALL

He stayed close to home to be near his grieving family, taking a job at a nearby gas works company. After two years on the job, William was overcome with gas fumes when testing a meter and ended up in the hospital where he underwent surgery for appendicitis. As he lay in the recovery room, he felt his life ebbing away. His body grew weaker and his mind grew dark; and then he heard the familiar voice saying, "I called you and you would not go." The words were repeated again and again. William's inner voice answered back, "Lord, if that is You, let me go back again to earth and I will preach our Gospel from the housetops and street corners."[15]

He was released from the hospital a few days later and began immediately to seek the Lord. He found a small, independent Baptist church that nurtured and prayed for him and then six months later ordained him an independent Baptist minister. William obtained a small tent and began to minister with great results. It was in June of 1933 at the age of twenty-four, that Branham held his first major tent revival. Three thousand people attended in one night. It was during this time that a supernatural manifestation occurred.

AN ANGEL VISITS 4,000 WHILE BAPTIZING IN THE OHIO RIVER

William was holding a special baptism service where he baptized 130 believers in the Ohio River. When he had baptized the seventeenth person, this is what William described happened: "A whirl came down from the heavens above, here come that light, shining down . . . it hung right over where I was at . . . and it like to a-scared me to death. The voice from

heaven said, 'As John the Baptist fore ran the first coming of Christ, you will forerun the second." Many of the four thousand that saw the supernatural light and heard the voice that came from heaven ran in fear! Others remained and fell in worship.[16]

Several months later, in the fall of that year, the people who attended those powerful meetings built a headquarters for William's anointed ministry calling it "Branham Tabernacle." From 1933 to 1946, Branham ministered at the Tabernacle while working at a secular job.

THE RUSHING WIND

He continued to preach at the Branham Tabernacle and have prophetic visions. No one seemed to understand him or the nature of his visions and he grew more restless. He did remarry during this time for his oldest child's sake and worked to provide for the family as a game warden in addition to preaching at the Tabernacle.

One spring day, in 1946, he came home for lunch and sat with a friend from work under a large maple tree. All of a sudden, according to Branham, "It seemed that the whole top of the tree let loose . . . it seemed like something came down from that tree like a great rushing wind." His wife came running out to see what the commotion was all about, and after getting a hold of his emotions, Branham shared all the past experiences he'd had with the wind rushing above him in the trees. Since he was a young child, a "mighty rushing wind" haunted him, spoke to him, and compelled him to seek God for answers.

He then told his wife that he was going to find out, once and for all what was behind this "wind" and recalled that he had said, "I told her and my child good-bye and warned her that if I didn't come back in a few days, perhaps I might never return."

A VISIT FROM AN ANGEL

Branham left for a cabin in a secluded place to pray and read the Bible. He cried out to the Lord to speak to him in some way. That night he noticed a light flickering in the room that began to spread across the floor and then grew into a ball of emerald fire shining on the floor which moved over the top of his head. Footsteps approached and he saw a large man dressed in a white robe coming toward him. The man spoke in a deep voice and said, "Fear not, I am sent from the presence of Almighty God to tell you that your peculiar life and your misunderstood ways have been to indicate that God has sent you to take a gift of divine healing to the people of the world. If you will be sincere, and can get the people to believe you, nothing shall stand before your prayer, not even cancer."

William humbly replied that he was so poor and uneducated no one would listen to him. The Angel gave him two gifts that he would use as signs to help the people believe. The first would be his ability to detect disease by a vibration in his left hand; and the other would be the word of knowledge revealing the secret sin hidden in a person's heart.

WALKING OUT THE CALLING

The following Sunday after returning home, Branham shared with his congregation what he had experienced. While he was speaking, someone handed him a telegram requesting that he come to St. Louis to pray for a gravely sick daughter. He quickly took up an offering for the train-fare and borrowed a suit of clothes. At midnight he boarded the train for St. Louis.

He arrived to find the girl dying from an unknown sickness. She was weak and wasting away, hoarse from crying out in pain. William was moved to tears and pulled away to seek the Lord privately about what to do. He saw the answer in a vision and waited until the conditions were just as he had seen them in the spirit. He asked the people present if they believed he was God's servant and directed them to do just he told them, doubting nothing. He proceeded to ask for several things and prayed according the vision the Lord had given him. Immediately the child was healed.

News spread quickly and the people of St. Louis asked Branham to return. In June of 1946 he conducted a twelve-day healing revival there where tremendous manifestations took place. The lame walked, the blind saw, the deaf heard, and the dead were raised. A woman who stood mocking outside dropped dead from a heart attack. Branham went out to pray for her and she revived praising God. The healings that took place were beyond count as Branham often stayed until 2:00 a.m. to pray for the sick.

From St. Louis he went on to Jonesboro, Arkansas, where 25,000 people attended the meetings. On one occasion, Branham went out to pray for a woman who had died in an ambulance outside the meeting hall. She sat up healed and Branham had to sneak out of the front of the ambulance under cover of disguise to return to the meeting.

RELENTLESS REVIVAL

1947 was a high profile year for Branham. In Arkansas he acquired his first campaign manager. Time published news of his campaigns as his ministry toured the western states. While in Portland, Oregon, T.L. and Daisy Osborn attended his meetings and were greatly influenced by what they witnessed. It has been said that this was the refreshing and refocus they needed to launch their world-changing international ministry.

This was also the year that Gordon Lindsey joined forces with Branham. Lindsey became his administrator and organized and promoted one of the greatest healing revivals to this day. Accompanied by Jack Moore, the "Union Campaign" joined the forces of the Oneness Pentecostals and the Full Gospel circles for a series of revival campaigns held throughout the Pacific Northwest and Canada. Branham was successful at avoiding doctrinal differences and leading thousands to salvation and healing. Reports stated that 1,500 souls were born again in a single service and as many as 35,000 healings were manifested during that stretch of ministry.

THE ORACLE HEALING MINISTRY

Often times in revival meetings William Branham would preach and then have to wait for the angel of the Lord to appear. William Branham would apologize to the audience and state time and time again that he was a man just like everyone else and that he could do nothing of himself and would try to explain the gift of God being the only reason he was able to move in the supernatural as he did. Then as quickly as he saw the angel of the Lord he would shift the meeting into high gear and begin to move in healing by vision.

I've watched videos of William Branham ministering and it is mind boggling. People lined up for prayer and stood in front of him. William called the next person in line and would say, *"Now don't be afraid of that presence, that is the Lord you are feeling."* As the person stepped forward for ministry William Branham launched into detailed visions of the person's life and began to minister to them out of that vision. He would be seemingly lost in another place as he revealed certain aspects of their life, city where they lived, their street address, their name and the names of those in their family and the specific condition that afflicted them. As he did this by the Holy Spirit of God he was never wrong and 100% of those who sought healing were healed every time. William Branham would come out of the vision and say, *"Of course I don't remember what was just said because it's gone from me now, but this was all true."* And then, the person he was ministering to raised his or her hand to confirm. Branham was completely under the power of the Holy Spirit to the point that he could remember no detail of what had occurred. He functioned as a modern day Oracle of God in his time, speaking as a mouthpiece for God.

WILLIAM BRANHAM WAS A FORERUNNER

When the angel first appeared to William Branham in the Ohio River he said, "As John the Baptist foreran the first coming of Christ, you will forerun the second coming of Christ." Forerunners demonstrate what is to come and what is being made available to all. They are the first. Branham never claimed to be anything more than this. He always stated that he was a brother and a friend just like everyone else. Even though there were many then and still today, that claim he was indeed John the Baptist or even Christ, he openly denied these statements and warned that if they continued, the Lord would take him home. Some say that Brother Branham got off into doctrinal error, which was never the case. He had strong beliefs on some issues but was never doctrinally incorrect. He remains today one of the most incredible post-modern, wonder-working Oracles of our time.

References:

William Branham, Maria Woodworth-Etter ... God's Generals

(God's Generals: The Revivalists, Roberts Liardon, 2008, Whitaker House, 109)

(God's Generals: The Revivalists, Roberts Liardon, 2008, Whitaker House, 114)

Chapter 4

RELEASING THE SUBATOMIC POWER OF PRAISE

There is a supernatural power that is released in praise that alters both the physical and non-physical realm. When the praises go up, the Glory comes down. It's that simple. If we are going to see the necessary breakthrough in our personal lives, churches, cities, regions and nations, then we need to understand the subatomic power of praise. Sound is an amazing force. Ray Hughes says, "A pair of 30 inch speakers connected to a tone generator can generate a note low enough to literally, physically move

a building off its foundation."[17] We are continually in the presence of ultrasonic and subsonic sound waves. *Ultra-* meaning "above," are waves above our threshold of hearing and *sub-* meaning "beneath," are waves beneath our threshold of hearing. Just because we can't physically hear them doesn't mean they don't exist. They do!

MAKING HISTORY – BREAKING THE SOUND BARRIER

Here's a quick bit of important history. The speed of sound is the distance traveled during a unit of time by a sound wave. In dry air at 20 °C (68° F), the speed of sound is 343.2 meters per second (1,126ft/s). This is 1,236 kilometers per hour (768 mph) or approximately one mile in five seconds. In aerodynamics, the *sound barrier* usually refers to the point at which an aircraft moves from transonic to supersonic speed. The term came into use during World War II when a number of aircrafts started to encounter the effects of compressibility, a collection of several unrelated aerodynamic effects that "struck" their planes like an impediment to further acceleration. By the 1950s, new aircraft designs started to routinely "break" the sound barrier.

U.S. Navy F/A-18 breaking the sound barrier. The white halo formed by condensed water droplets is thought to result from a drop in air pressure around the aircraft at transonic speeds.

Some common whips such as the bullwhip or spare-whip are able to move faster than sound: the tip of the whip breaks the sound barrier and causes a sharp crack—literally a sonic boom. Firearms since the 19th century have generally had a supersonic muzzle velocity.

It was in the X-1 that Chuck Yeager was credited with being the first man to break the sound barrier in level flight on 14 October 1947, flying at an altitude of 45,000 ft (13.7 km). He had christened his plane the *Glamorous Glennis*. The rocket-powered aircraft was launched from the bomb bay of a specially modified B-29 and glided to a landing on a runway.

Prior to Chuck Yeager's success, there were many failed attempts to break the sound barrier most of which resulted in fatal or near fatal crashes. As the plane would reach the speed of sound, water molecules would form at the nose of the craft causing external pressure and push the aircraft backward. Vibration would cause the plane to begin to break up and nose dive or veer off uncontrolled resulting in tragedy.[18]

THE SONIC BOOM

To break the sound barrier one would have to push through the resistance at the nose of the plane by thrusting forward. As the plane would begin to break the barrier, water vapor and pressure would move to the tail of the craft and as full penetration would occur, the barrier of resistance would become the catalyst of *Sonic Thrust* causing it to catapult forward and create what is known today as the *Sonic Boom*.

At the point of reaching the sound barrier one can either release the pressure and fall back where it is comfortable and predictable, or one can by thrust forward to where few have gone before and BREAK THROUGH into the sonic boom level.

THE SUBATOMIC POWER OF PRAISE

There is a supernatural power that is released in praise that alters both the physical and non-physical realm. When the praises go up, the Glory comes down. It's that simple. If we are going to see breakthrough in our personal lives, churches, cities, regions and nations, then we need to understand the subatomic power of praise.

Praise means *to commend, to applaud or magnify*. For the Christian, praise to God is an expression of worship, lifting-up and glorifying the Lord. It is an expression of humbling ourselves and centering our attention upon the Lord with heart-felt expressions of love, adoration and thanksgiving. High praises bring our spirit into a pinnacle of fellowship and intimacy between ourselves and God — it magnifies our awareness of our spiritual union with the Most High God. Praise transports us into the realm of the supernatural and into the power of God. *"Blessed is the people that know the joyful sound: they shall walk, O LORD, in the light of thy countenance"* (Ps. 89:15, KJV).

There are many actions involved with praise to God—verbal expressions of adoration and thanksgiving, singing, playing instruments, shouting, dancing, lifting or clapping our hands. Unpretentious praise and worship pleases the Lord. According to Scripture, the various expressions of praise bring blessing to the Lord. He eagerly awaits the fragrance of our affections, desiring to manifest His sweet presence and power in our midst. *"The true worshipers shall worship the Father in spirit and in truth: for the Father seeks such to worship him"* (John 4:23).

CREATING A CULTURE OF PRAISE

All too often, praise to God is something that many people leave at church, an event that happens only when they come together with other Christians. However, praise should be a part of a believer's lifestyle, intermingled as a part of their daily prayer-life—at work, in the car, at home in bed, or anywhere—praise to the Lord brings the refreshing of the Lord's presence, along with His power and anointing. *"I will bless the LORD at all times: his praise shall continually be in my mouth"* (Ps. 34:1).

Praise is an expression of faith, and a declaration and realization that God is always with us, and is in control of the outcome of all our circumstances (see Rom. 8:28). Praise is a "sacrifice," something that we offer to God sacrificially, not just because we feel like it, but because we believe in Him and wish to please Him. *"By Him therefore let us offer the sacrifice of praise to God continually, that is, the fruit of our lips giving thanks to his name"* (Heb. 13:15).

SONIC VIBRATION

Science confirms that every created thing is made up of sound waves that are constantly spinning at different intervals, forming objects in matter of various densities both small and great. We also understand sound as a power, that when cranked up to a certain level or frequency, it will break or crush glass or break windows in a house. All sound and color and images are wavelengths that move by vibration and are a power that have substance.

That being said, we need to understand that every attitude carries its own power and vibration which is recognizable in the realm of the spirit. It is not just an attitude… it is a force that wraps itself around a person like a coat that continually pulls a person deeper into its power until they are completely overtaken by it—whether for good or bad. Every attitude we release is filled with powerful vibrations wrapping themselves around us like a garment, further enveloping us into its cocoon-like power.

> *For by your words you will be justified and acquitted [set free], and by your words you will be condemned and sentenced [condemned]…* (Matt. 12:37).

Jesus was saying that the words we wrap ourselves in will either set us free or imprison us here in this life and in eternity to come!

> *Death and life are in the power of the tongue, and they who indulge in it shall eat the fruit of it [for death or life]* (Prov. 18:21).

PRAISE SHATTERS THE ENEMY

Since praise manifests God's presence, we also know that praise repels the presence of the enemy, Satan. An atmosphere that is filled with the sincere worship and praise of God's people will send the enemy running. For in the presence of the Lord there is fullness of joy. Satan cannot contend with or find remedy for the all-encompassing presence of God. He must flee…. Satan cannot stand the manifest presence of God. Every time the devil encountered the presence of Jesus in Scripture, he immediately recognized, and publicly attested to, the supreme majesty and power of Jesus Christ.

The demons have always begged for mercy from Him to not torment them before their time. So it is with us.

As we cultivate an environment of the Glory of God through High Praises the enemy will run from us, demons will automatically scatter, sickness and disease will lose their grip as they are demonically induced and will eventually fall away. So the key to the end-time church is to become a praising people that stops at nothing short of the manifest presence of Jesus Christ in our midst and the power of the Holy Ghost presence that will drive every inferior dimension of sickness and disease from our midst through the unashamed, uplifted faces of a family of sons and daughters that have full confidence born out of a pure revelation that He longs to be with us and dwell in our midst. This kind of thinking is dangerous for the devil to see happening in the saints of God. As the Presence of God comes, the *veil is stripped away and we are being transfigured from one degree of Glory and revelation to another by the Lord who is that Spirit* (see 2 Cor. 3:18).

Satan becomes powerless to stop the renewal of the mind and the flow of revelation that comes to transform the person. He fears the power of the name of Jesus, and runs from the presence of the Lord.

> *Whoso offers praise glorifies me: and to him that orders his conversation aright will I show the salvation of God* (Ps. 50:23).

When the children of Judah found themselves outnumbered by the hostile armies of Ammon, Moab, and mount Seir, King Jehoshaphat and all the people sought the Lord for His help. The Lord assured the people that this would be His battle. He told them to go out against them, and He would do the fighting for them. So what did the children of Judah do? Being a people of praise (Judah actually means praise), and knowing that God manifests His power through praise, they sent their army against their enemies, led by the praisers!

So, on they went, ahead of the army declaring, "Praise the Lord, for His mercy endures forever!" And the Scripture says, *"...when they began to sing and to praise, the LORD set ambushments against the children of Ammon, Moab, and mount Seir, which were come against Judah; and they were smitten"* (2 Chron. 20:22).

When God's people begin to praise His name, it sends the enemy running! I challenge you to become a person of praise, and you will experience the release of the power of God!

RELEASING THE GOD SOUND

> *But You are holy, O You Who dwell in [the holy place where] the praises of Israel [are offered]* (Ps. 22:3).

Praising God means adoring Him, honoring Him, and exalting Him, and He takes delight in the praise of the saints. To "Praise" is to *commend the worth of, express approval or admiration of.*

> *Enter into his gates with thanksgiving, and into his courts with praise: be thankful unto him, and bless his name* (Ps.100:4).

We should always come into the presence of God with praise and thanksgiving. God lives in the midst of our praises—if you want God to come close—praise Him.

In chapter 2, I touched on the power that was released from heaven with Paul and Silas. Paul cast a spirit of divination out of a woman of Thyatira, and when her masters saw that they would no longer make gain from her, they caught Paul and Silas and brought them before the rulers, and when they had beaten them, they cast them in prison.

> *But about midnight, as Paul and Silas were praying and singing hymns of praise to God, and the [other] prisoners were listening to*

*them, Suddenly there was a great earthquake, so that the very founda-
tions of the prison were shaken; and at once all the doors were opened
and everyone's shackles were unfastened* (Acts 16:25-26).

Paul and Silas understood what it took to change their circumstances. Praise
and thanksgiving released a floodgate of power from the unseen realm of
Glory that manifested in the natural. That power created an earthquake
that shook the very foundation of the prison and resulting in everyone's
shackles falling off. Praise produced a sonic wave of God-Sound.

THE STONES CRY OUT

When Jesus entered into Jerusalem on Palm Sunday, the people gathered
to praise God for all the great miracles they had seen Jesus perform. The
religious leaders were there as well and demanded that the people stop
praising. Jesus said if these people keep silent the very stones will cry out
in praise!

> *As He was approaching [the city], at the descent of the Mount of Ol-
> ives, **the whole crowd of the disciples began to rejoice and to praise
> God [extolling Him exultantly and] loudly for all the mighty mir-
> acles and works of power that they had witnessed,** Crying, Blessed
> (celebrated with praises) is the King Who comes in the name of the
> Lord! Peace in heaven freedom there from all the distresses that are
> experienced as the result of sin] and glory (majesty and splendor) in
> the highest [heaven]! And some of the Pharisees from the throng said
> to Jesus, Teacher, reprove Your disciples! He replied, I tell you that if
> these keep silent, the very stones will cry out* (Luke 19:35-40, empha-
> sis mine).

The stones have ears and memory and will cry out! Before entering into
the Promised Land, Joshua recounted the covenant between the people
and the Lord:

And Joshua wrote these words in the Book of the Law of God; and he took a great stone and set it up there under an oak that was in [the court of] the sanctuary of the Lord. And Joshua said to all the people, See, **this stone shall be a witness against us, for it has "heard all the words" the Lord spoke to us;** *so it shall be a witness against you, lest [afterward] you lie (pretend) and deny your God* (Josh. 24:27-28, emphasis mine).

JEHOSHAPHAT'S VICTORY THROUGH PRAISE

A great multitude came against Jehoshaphat to battle, and he set himself to seek God, and proclaimed a fast; God heard and answered, *"Be not afraid, nor dismayed by reason of this great multitude; for the battle is not yours, but God's... Tomorrow go ye out against them... ye shall not need to fight in this battle: set yourselves, stand ye still, and see the salvation of the Lord with you..."* (1 Chron. 20:15-17, KJV).

> *When he had consulted with the people, he appointed singers to sing to the Lord and praise Him in their holy [priestly] garments as they went out before the army, saying, Give thanks to the Lord, for His mercy and loving-kindness endure forever! And when they began to sing and to praise, the Lord set ambushments against the men of Ammon, Moab, and Mount Seir who had come against Judah, and they were [self-] slaughtered...* (2 Chron. 20:21-22).

THE RUAH SHOUT

The Hebrew word "Ruah," which is *the very breath of God,* can also be translated, *Shout.* It is the same word used in Psalm 100:1 and Psalm 95:1 and translated *shout joyfully* and *make a joyful noise.* Other meanings include *battle cry, shout of triumph,* and *sound an alarm.* Ruah was used to denote any shout of joy or praise. In fact in public worship it would denote praise of the most animated kind, which always required a body function.

One of those words is the word "Shabach" which means to *shout in a loud address or tone*. The priest blew the trumpets; the people raised a great shout of triumph, and praise; God's presence and power came down; and the walls of Jericho fell flat. When the praise went up the presence came down. It's interesting to note that it is the very breath of God (Ruah) that comes through the mouths of His people in the shout. He is the very breath (Ruah) of life living in us. When we shout unto God, it is literally God's breath and sound that are being exhaled into the atmosphere. Every created living thing recognizes the God-Sound vibration and responds.

A GREAT VIBRATION IN HEAVEN

When heaven shouts in praise - the angels and spiritual creatures, the saints who have gone before us and form the great cloud of witnesses – their combined God-Sound is like a mighty roar, like the boom of many pounding waves. This shout in heaven actually creates a vibration (a sound wave) that, when it collides with the natural realm, shakes the very foundations of the earth.

THE TANZANIA SHOUT

In 2008, I took a team with me to Tanzania, Africa for a Global Fire Crusade. I had done many crusades but this one was going to be different. We were expecting a crowd of nearly 100,000 and we were all excited. We planned to be in Tanzania after the rainy season to assure success so our team was pumped and ready. On the first night of the five-night crusade few people had shown up, not the more than 3,000. Toward the end of three hours of worship, monsoon-looking rain clouds began to appear. Suddenly, the rain poured down. I noticed black ravens flying overhead as people were scrambling to pick up their belongings and children and run for cover. I said to myself, "Somebody is praying, and it's not the Christians." Without thinking, I screamed into the microphone, "Not on my crusade," and commanded the rain clouds to stop in Jesus name. As quickly as these monsoon clouds rolled in, they left. That night we had a crusade and many great miracles happened. People gave their lives to Jesus Christ as Kingdom power and authority was manifesting.

The Lord told me on the first night of the crusade, "Jeff, if you can get the people to give Me a shout of praise each night I will do great miracles." So before I preached I would get the people to release a shout of praise in the crowd that when released was like a sonic wave of sound that went up into the heavens and returned like a supernatural sonic boom upon the people resulting in mass miracles. I barely had time to preach. As the praises went up, the Glory came down. People were getting up out of their wheelchairs. I saw tumors dissolving, blind eyes opening, crippled babies walking, it was amazing! And after they got healed, they would give their lives to Jesus. Each night as we shouted, biblical type miracles would occur and the crowds would grow as word spread throughout the city.

By the fifth night, approximately 80,000 people crowded the soccer field. It was a beautiful night in Tanzania. The sun was just setting over the horizon casting a shadow on the mountains in the background. As I stood up to preach, I heard the Lord say to me, "Jeff you better hurry up."

I asked, "What do you mean Lord?" As I looked over the crowd of people, I saw flaming lights coming from around each side of the large mountain. I heard the Lord say to me again, "Jeff... you better hurry up!" I could see through the eyes of my spirit, chariots of fire descending from around the mountain coming toward the people.

I hurried the people to their feet and said, "Tonight Jesus Christ is going to do great miracles, but first we are going to give Him a shout of praise!" The Lord told me if I could get these Muslim people to give Him praise, He would do great miracles. People who had received miracles from the previous nights brought their families and friends as the spreading reports of the many miracles drew their curiosity. Most knew the drill. I hurried the people to stand in the soccer field and on the count of three with the band we released a corporate shout of praise to Jesus Christ. As we did, those angelic chariots of fire descended upon the people resulting in mass deliverance. People dropped to the ground under the power of heaven as devils manifested. I had never seen anything like this in my life. This region was a satanic hot bed of ritualistic activity and many were being instantly delivered. The city elders told me they have had in many great evangelists and hosted many crusades, but never had they seen these kinds of miracles from a first time evangelist. Thousands were instantly healed and immediately responded to salvation.

THE HIGH PRAISES OF GOD

Praise is one of the highest weapons the believer possesses. Through praise, battles have been won and nations conquered. David wrote:

> *Let the high praises of God be in their throats and a two-edged sword in their hands, To wreak vengeance upon the nations and chastisement upon the peoples, To bind their kings with chains, and their nobles with fetters of iron, To execute upon them the judgment written. He [the Lord] is the honor of all His saints. Praise the Lord! (Hallelujah!) (Ps. 149:6-9).*

Let the "High Praises" of God be in your mouth—not the low praises. High praises are the release of thanksgiving and honor given directly to the Lord Jesus Christ. When we give Him the Glory *due His name* and begin to sing directly to Him instead of about Him, He comes with all of His Glory. As the high praises are in our mouths, the double edged sword is automatically in our hands, to wreak vengeance upon nations, punishment upon enemies, to bind kings (demonic) with chains and fetters, and to execute judgment. For the Lord is the honor of all His saints! When the praises go up, the Glory comes down and every enemy of the saints is rendered powerless. Sickness, disease, poverty, lack must all bow to the mighty name of Jesus Christ.

THE JOYFUL SOUND

David wrote about many types of praise including high praises and joyful sounds. These are not just nice, descriptive words—they are powerful.

> *Blessed (happy, fortunate, to be envied) are the people who know the joyful sound [who understand and appreciate the spiritual blessings symbolized by the feasts]; they walk, O Lord, in the light and favor of Your countenance! In Your name they rejoice all the day, and in Your righteousness they are exalted. For You are the glory of their strength [their proud adornment], and by Your favor our horn is exalted and we walk with uplifted faces! (Ps. 89:15-17, AMP)*

Blessed are those who know the "Joyful Sound." What is the joyful sound? It's the sound of High Praise that brings the transforming Glory of God! In the joyful sound, God's friends rejoice all day long, for the Lord is their strength and they can walk with their faces lifted toward Him with no shame.

The enemy cannot touch the warring praising saint, for his attention is on the loveliness and sweet attractiveness of the Lord and they walk in the Light of the Glory of God. No devil can follow you there! With our attitudes we are constantly attracting one of two kingdoms; either the Kingdom of light or the kingdom of darkness. All too often we are looking for some kind of super-spiritual answer or remedy to deliver us from our condition, when all we need to do is simply worship and praise our way through it.

THE CLOAK OF THANKSGIVING

Isaiah prophesied to a generation that was yet to come. He said the Spirit of the Lord is upon us:

> *To grant [consolation and joy] to those who mourn in Zion—to give*

*them an ornament (a garland or diadem) of beauty instead of ashes,
the oil of joy instead of mourning, the garment [expressive] of praise
instead of a heavy, burdened, and failing spirit...* (Isa. 61:3).

The Hebrew word for "garment" here is *mattah*, which means *to wrap oneself in or to veil oneself*. When we choose to put on the garment of praise we begin to wrap ourselves in the power and light of that garment, which destroys the spirit of heaviness.

The Hebrew word for "praise" is *hallal*, which means to *shine forth with sound and color*. When we begin to praise, we shine with *light and color and sound*. So when we choose to praise, we wrap ourselves in a supernatural garment of power and light which flows with an unstoppable force that destroys the spirit of heaviness. When we choose to be thankful, we are filled with light, and depression, sadness, and despair from the demonic realm are cut off. [19]

Chapter 5

BECOMING A GATEWAY OF THE SUPERNATURAL REALM

SUPERNATURAL GATEWAYS OF LIGHT

Before we look at this chapter, I believe it's important for us to understand what it means to become a gateway of the Supernatural realm. The life of Jesus was filled with extraordinary events that reach far beyond what we would call the norm of the day. The disciples also moved in the Exousia power that flowed from the mantle of the Spirit of the Lord that rested on Jesus' life as He demonstrated to them what it meant to become a gateway in both the natural and spiritual mind. In Matthew 16:13-17 Jesus asked His disciples:

> *Who do people say that the Son of Man is? And they answered, Some say John the Baptist; others say Elijah; and others Jeremiah or one of the prophets. He said to them, But who do you [yourselves] say that I am? Simon Peter replied, You are the Christ, the Son of the living God. And Jesus said to him, Blessed (happy, fortunate, and to be envied) are you, Simon Bar-Jonah. For flesh and blood [men] have not revealed this to you, but My Father Who is in heaven.*

Four verses later Peter has another revelation after Jesus told them plainly He would have to go to the cross:

Then Peter took Him aside to speak to Him privately and began to reprove and charge Him sharply, saying, God forbid, Lord! This must never happen to You! But Jesus turned away from Peter and said to him, Get behind Me, Satan! You are in My way [an offense and a hindrance and a snare to Me]; for you are minding what partakes not of the nature and quality of God, but of men (Matt. 16:22-23).

Peter moved from being a gateway of revelation from the Father in one moment to becoming a gateway of darkness the next, to which the Lord literally said to him, *"...get behind Me, Satan!"* How could this be? From Holy Ghost revelation to Satanic information in less than 60 seconds!

In truth, we all reveal one of two minds, either the natural mind or the mind of the Spirit. Jesus was our great example. He was the Firstborn among many brothers. He was in complete union with the Father at all times. As a result, He turned water into wine, had Peter pull a coin out of a fish's mouth, multiplied five loaves of bread and two small fish feeding five thousand men, not including women and children, walked on water, spoke to fig trees and storms and they obeyed Him, and demons acknowledged Him and ran from His presence! The supernatural events were so numerous they couldn't even all be recorded. These testimonies were given us as an example so we would know by certainty what is available and rightfully ours to walk in when rightly connected with God. Jesus plainly told us:

I assure you, and most solemnly I tell you, if anyone steadfastly believes in Me, he will himself be able to do the things that I do; and he will do even greater things than these, because I go to the Father (John 14:12).

THE SUPERNATURAL STONES OF SEATTLE

The testimony you are about to read is the accurate account of events as they occurred at Transformation Center Church International in Seattle,

Washington. I'm adding this testimony to further illustrate what it means to become a supernatural gateway of Light. The Lord is calling the church into a place of such union with Him that signs like these will be the norm and not the exception. I pray that you will honor the Glory of God as you read the testimony of Andrey Shapovalov, pastor of TCCI.

ANDREY SHAPOVALOV

Pastor Andrey Shapovalov
Transformation Center Church International
Seattle, Washington

It was in the in the summer of 2009 when we first had Jeff Jansen come to the Transformation Center Church in Seattle, Washington. Our meeting was ordained of God from the start. Jeff was scheduled to be in another meeting in the Seattle area that had cancelled. The night of the cancellation, Jennifer Martin, wife of Munday Martin, had a unique dream with Jeff in it. In the dream she saw a large rocket getting ready to take off. On the two visible fins of the rocket was an American flag and a Russian flag. Printed on the side of the rocket was the word "YOUGOTA 827," which we interpreted to be a Russian city somewhere. Jennifer called Jeff and told him the dream. Later that day, Jeff received a phone call from the Transformation Center asking him to come there instead. We told Jeff we were a Russian church and he accepted the invitation based on the dream. We picked Jeff up from the airport, ate lunch and then headed for the church. Along the way we discussed the details of the "YOUGOTA 827" dream and what it could possibly mean, as we could not find any information on it as a Russian city. As we pulled up to the building someone screamed, "Look! Our address is 827!" Then it became clear, "You – go - ta - 827" the Russian church! We all laughed with excitement. The Lord was up to something.

Immediately Jeff began to tell us things about who we were and where we were going. Our relationship was a hit from the start. I feel it important to tell you that going back to my teen years I had witnessed many incredible displays of the presence of God with friends—we encountered the Lord in many wonderful ways. We would be swept away into the Glory of God for extended periods of time—sometimes up to eight hours or more! These encounters I believed prepared me and our church for what we were about to receive in this season at TCCI.

Jeff told us that God was making our church a house for His Glory. He said that the feathers would start coming as a sign, and that the gemstones would be coming just like in Coeur d'Alene, Idaho. Jeff said that he saw that the Glory of God that was over Coeur d'Alene, Idaho at one time had moved over Seattle, Washington and that we were to make room and get ready for God. As Jeff was leaving that weekend he gave Ally Piatnitsky a gemstone from his collection and said this would be the first of many.

GET READY FOR THE NEW

Later that year in November the feathers came into our meetings, houses, cars, work places just as we were told. Testimonies would come from our affiliate covenant churches from all around Europe as they were connected to us globally. Then in January 2010, Jeff came back for a Glory Explosion conference and everything changed. The very first night Jeff asked us if we believed God would fill peoples teeth with gold. The whole church shouted, "Yes!"

Then Jeff said, "I've even seen God put a diamond in a gold tooth in a person's mouth... do you believe that God would do that?"

Again the whole church shouted, "Yes, we believe that!"

He said again, "I've even see God put a ruby in a gold tooth in a mouth, do you believe that God would do that?"

The church exploded with an overwhelming, "Yes! We believe God can do anything!" There were great miracles that night but the greatest of miracles were yet to come.

Lana Golodyuk

On Sunday morning, the last session, powerful waves of the Glory of God came into the service; waves that were felt by all. Right toward the end of the preaching Lana Golodyuk, one of our leaders, was worshipping when she was hit with what she said described as a "ball of fire." Lana said it was so powerful that when it hit her, she bent over causing her teeth to come together and her back tooth cracked in two. She said she could feel the heat from the fire still in her stomach and her throat, mouth and tongue became extremely dry. Lana asked her husband for water and was feeling something rolling around in the back of her mouth. She thought, "My tooth cracked in two." Then Lana spit what she thought was her tooth into her husband's hand only to see that it was a two-karat diamond! Lana screamed and fell to the floor and the church exploded with wonder and amazement. Jeff said diamonds were coming in the mouth; even still, we were all shocked.

From that time to the present, almost two years ago, we have received over 45 stones of various sizes, colors and shapes from Lana's mouth. Every time a stone would come in a meeting it either comes to confirm the Word that is being preached or as a sign to a vision that has come. Something new was birthed into the ministry and we were excited about what could possibly be coming next. We do not chase after signs and wonders, they come to confirm what God is already doing or is about to do. The Word of God says that attesting signs follow them that believe (see Mark 16:17).

Gateways of Glory

These stones that Andrey testified about come from the Glory realm by the Spirit of God and manifest in the natural through Gateways of Glory. We are Glory containers in the earth. We were designed by God to carry His Glory to the nations. Sometimes, as in this case, the stones come in the mouth. Sometimes they come through the skin, or appear on the ground.

I have a friend who had a stone come out through the palm of his hand in a meeting I was doing with Charlie Robinson in Hastings, New Zealand. He felt something uncomfortable in the palm of his hand as he was paging through his Bible, only to open his hand and literally, watch as the one-karat stone "popped up from under his skin into his hand." He was shocked. It came from the "inside out." We are Glory carriers, Glory containers. Jesus said that the Kingdom of God is in you and all around you (see Luke 17:23, AMP).

BECOMING A THRONE OF HONOR & GLORY

As I mentioned in Chapter 2, I want to look a little deeper into the Isaiah 22:22-23, Key of David principle. It relates to the descending Throne of God that rests not only over our cities and regions, but over our very lives. As we offer up High Praises to God, we connect on a level far greater than we realize. We literally become Supernatural Gateways of Light that the Glory of God flows through bringing power, revelation, miracles and everything needed for that particular atmosphere. Let's look again at the key of David principle as it relates to the descending Throne of God that rests not only over our cities and regions, but over our very lives.

> *And the key of the house of David I will lay upon his shoulder; he shall open and no one shall shut, he shall shut and no one shall open. And I will fasten him like a peg or nail in a firm place; and he will become a throne of honor and glory to his father's*

house. And *they will hang on him the honor and the whole weight of [responsibility for] his father's house: the offspring and issue [of the family, high and low], every small vessel, from the cups even to all the flasks and big bulging bottles* (Isa. 22:22-23, emphasis mine).

Isaiah foresaw a company of believers who would be like a peg or a nail in a firm place, like a peg that someone would use to hang a cloak or a mantle on *and he will become a throne of honor and glory to his father's house.*

This Glory Company will not only possess the keys of the Kingdom, but will understand how to use them. They will be able to speak in every situation both to the natural and the supernatural realm and be able to open doors that no man can shut, and shut doors that no one can open. These believers will move with unlimited anointing and authority because they possess revelation knowledge of the blueprints of heaven with an understanding of their position and inheritance in the Kingdom.

The passage says that he will become a *Throne of Honor and Glory* in His Father's House. Who will become a THRONE of HONOR and GLORY? The one on whom the Key to the House of David rests. He will become unmovable to the world and will be fastened like a nail in a firm place. This individual will become a supernatural gateway of heaven and even a *Throne!* I'm telling you that the worshipping Sons of God in these last days will literally become the Throne that the Lord Jesus Christ rests upon to reveal His Kingdom of power and Glory! Try preaching that in some of the mainline denominational churches!

Nonetheless, it is the truth! Psalm 122 says that *He is enthroned upon the praises of Israel.*

The throne of God literally rests on the praises of His people. What does that look like? When we begin to praise God with the understanding that He is the great King of heaven and worship Him with this attitude and reality, the Bible says that His throne will literally be built upon and come to rest on top of those praises. Wherever the high praises of God are found on the earth, this is where the Throne of God will rest. Wherever the Throne of God is, the King is. Wherever the King is… there is a Kingdom. Wherever the Kingdom is—the angels are—and all of the resources of the government of that domain are present in reality.

ANGELS MOVING THROUGH SUPERNATURAL GATES

Back in 2005, I was in a Glory Explosion meeting in Yakima, Washington with Randy DeMain and several other ministry friends. In the meeting I noticed something happening in the room, near a table of showbread in the front of the church. It appeared to be a smoke ring swirling above the table that turned into what looked like a smoke doorway of some sort. I was standing next to Randy and was just getting ready to point it out to him when he grabbed my arm and said, "Hey Jeff look over there… a portal is opening up." As soon as he said this, out came this beautiful angel. I need to emphasis here that I am very cautious when it comes to talking about the angelic realm. We need to make sure that we always speak the truth and with the utmost respect, giving accurate details and information as they occur. Now, I want to leave off here and rewind to a few days prior to the Yakima meeting and share another encounter that will help bring this into focus.

The Spirit of Wisdom

Two days prior to this event in Yakima, Washington the Lord woke me up at 4:00 a.m. to pray. As I was sitting in my chair, I had an encounter from heaven. While praying I had a visitation from the Spirit of Wisdom who came and spoke to me out of the book of Proverbs chapter 8. I never thought of Wisdom as being female in appearance, but the truth of the matter is she is.

Does not wisdom call... besides the gates, at the opening to the city, at the entrance of the doors, she cries out... (Prov. 8:1-2, NASB).

For 45 minutes, Wisdom spoke with me about details of creation and how she was there in the beginning with the Lord as a *"master builder"* over all His works. Wisdom told me how she applauded all of the works of His hands and that it was by her (Wisdom) that a house was built. She told me that all of God's children were there along with the angels in the beginning and how all were amazed and praising God for all of the wonderful works of creation.

Wisdom then told me, "Jeff, you were there... remember?"

Honestly I couldn't remember anything. I was too absorbed in the details of what was happening before me. To date, I can tell you that this is one of the most interactive and incredible encounters I've ever experienced.

Wisdom then said, "*Jeff, to get Wisdom is better than Rubies, and today you are being given a new measure of Wisdom.*"

After Wisdom had finished speaking, I noticed two other large angels present in the background. Each of them had scrolls in their hands that were rolled up—they looked like white leather and appeared to have writing on both sides. The first angel approached me. Involuntarily, I opened my mouth as he crammed this large, four-foot scroll down my throat. The second angel did the same thing. I felt like I was simply along for the ride and had to keep telling myself not to think.

When the two angels were finished, another beautiful angel came into view. It was the same angel I would later see in Yakima, Washington. Somehow I instinctively knew to hold out my right hand and when I did the angel carefully placed in it a 50-karat Ruby! Then I heard again what Wisdom told me, *"To get Wisdom is better than rubies."*

I kept thinking to myself, "What's happening to me? Was I dreaming this or was it real?"

Now, fast-forward to the meeting in Yakima. Here I was with my friend Randy DeMain and the angel had just come through the smoke door. It was the same angel that brought me the 50-karat ruby two days before. As the angel came through the door, all were intensely worshipping in the room with hands raised. I too, had my hands raised, but when I recognized the angel I lowered my right hand and held it open! I had seen this before in a vision. I was thinking, *"Here it comes, my 50-karat Ruby!"* I know it must have looked kind of foolish but I had to obey the vision. The interesting thing is the angel walked right past Randy and me, and went over to another man who was on his knees worshipping with his hands upheld. Then the angel dropped that 50-karat Ruby into his hand. When the man felt the ruby, he opened his eyes, saw the angel, and screamed as loud as he could. Immediately, the angel disappeared and he was left alone with people standing all around him snapping pictures. I knew exactly what had just happened. As I walked over there and looked, sure enough, there it was, the 50-karat Ruby. I was shocked. I said, *"Lord, what are You doing? What is this all about?"* I was happy and rejoicing, but I couldn't help thinking, *"That was my 50-karat ruby!"*

As I was walking back to my seat, the Lord told this man, *"This is Jeff's stone, go and give it to him."* As he was on his way to give it to me, people were still taking photographs of the stone in his open hand. As he approached me, something happened. His hand began to vibrate and right in front of everyone the stone multiplied. Now there were TWO 50-karat stones in his hand. He handed me the original stone that the angel brought for me, and he kept the other. What an amazing set of circumstances. We were all shocked and amazed at what was taking place. This angel that I had seen two days prior gave me a 50-karat stone in the realm of the spirit had now just delivered it hand to hand.

ANGELS ASCENDING AND DESCENDING

In John 1, Jesus told Nathaniel that he would see the angels constantly moving up and down out of the gateways between heaven and earth like Jacob did in Genesis 28 when he saw heaven open with angels ascending and descending on a ladder:

> *Jesus replied, "Because I said to you, I saw you beneath the fig tree, do you believe in and rely on and trust in Me? You shall see greater things than this!" Then He said to him, "I assure you, most solemnly I tell you all, you shall see heaven opened, and the angels of God ascending and descending upon the Son of Man"* (John 1:50-51).

When we speak the Word of God we become a Word Gate that the angels move upon to do the Mighty works of the Lord.

> *Praise the LORD, you his angels, you mighty ones who do his bidding, who obey his word* (Ps. 103:20).

As the anointed *Rhema* Word of the Lord comes out of our mouths in ministry, the angels take that anointed Word and instantly perform or fulfill it as a messenger or agent of God. The angels work with the sons and daughters of God in doing miracles and healing, even in bringing revelation and information out of the realm of Glory. So what does that look like? Angels take the anointed Word of God as it comes out of your mouth and execute it. You have the authority of the Kingdom of God and it surrounds you even as you speak. Jesus said:

> *For behold, the kingdom of God is within you [in your hearts] and among you [surrounding you]* (Luke 17:21).

What does it look like to have the Kingdom of God in you and constantly surrounding you? What does it look like to become a "Throne of Honor?" What does it look like to be united with the Lord as one-Spirit with Him as Paul mentioned in 1 Corinthians 6:17, *"But the person who is united to the Lord becomes one spirit with Him"*?

Think about that! We are One with Him! What type of human being does that make you? It makes you a *"God-like one in the earth!"* You literally become a GATEWAY OF LIGHT in the earth. Everything in the spirit world sees you. Angels as well as demons know who you are. They see the Light of God flowing through your spirit-man as a vessel, a portal, a supernatural highway of the Kingdom of God. We become a THRONE and there is One Who sits on that Throne. Do you get it? Jesus wasn't kidding when He said:

> *If a person [really] loves Me, he will keep My word [obey My teaching]; and My Father will love him, and We will come to him and make Our home (abode, special dwelling place) with him* (John 14:23).

Jesus told Nathaniel that we, too, can become a gateway for the supernatural:

> *Because I said to you, I saw you beneath the fig tree, do you believe in and rely on and trust in Me? You shall see greater things than this! Then He said to him, "I assure you, most solemnly I tell you all, you shall see heaven opened, and the angels of God ascending and descending upon the Son of Man"* (John 1:50-51)!

When we are connected with heaven, we literally become a gateway for the supernatural to manifest in and around us. Heaven moves up and down upon us releasing signs wonders and miracles with our cooperation. God is looking for an end time army to arise with this revelation. And I fully believe we are the generation. There is a fresh sound being released from heaven with incredible power and Glory that the world has never seen, and it is falling on individuals that will bring it to the nations of the earth.

IMAGINATION IS THE GATEWAY TO THE SUPERNATURAL

Here is another truth that is important for us to understand as it relates to us becoming living gateways of the Supernatural: Thoughts are seeds, and when planted in the proper soil, they will reproduce after their own kind. Your thought life is just as real as when you speak. Words are verbalized thoughts. When thoughts are held close to the heart and mixed with passion and strong desire, a spiritual heat causes that seed to spin into life — and according to the Creation Law of Reproduction, they will produce after their own kind.

This is what is meant by Proverbs 23:7, "*As a man thinks in his heart so is he....*" We have this Godlike component to create like He did. It all starts in the thoughts and the imagination. The imagination is the gateway to the supernatural — it is the door to the spirit realm. What you think upon will manifest in the natural!

You don't even have to be a Christian for this to operate. There are many people doing things illegally by this principle alone. Remember, the Human Mind is a great earthly power as we are made in the very image of God. This law is Universal and cannot be changed.

THOUGHTS THAT BIRTH FROM PASSION

Jesus goes on to reveal the power of your thoughts to create life:

> *For this reason I am telling you, whatever you ask for in prayer, believe (trust and be confident) that it is granted to you, and you will [get it]* (Mark 11:24).

Desire is a very powerful emotion. Jesus is saying desire, believe, speak and you will have. Our thoughts are not just thoughts that nobody hears. They are the seeds of desire that produce and chart the course of our present and future life. If thoughts are seeds, and they are, we must understand how they are planted.

When your thoughts connect with desire in the emotions, the power of light is released. If you can hold your thoughts until they are connected with your emotions or feelings or desire, when they connect they become a power—a life and a light. This is the principle and power of agreement inherent in Mathew 18:19, "*Again, I tell you that if two of you… agree about anything… it will be done for you…*" (NIV).

When your emotions agree with your thinking—it shall be done—that's the power of union. As I wrote about in my previous book, *Glory Rising*, this is a spiritual law: The Creation Law of Reproduction[20]. It cannot be stopped. Take, for example, the seemingly unstoppable force of fear. Fear is just a thought until it connects with your emotions. You may hear a noise outside your home at night. For a moment your mind is flooded with thoughts about what that noise could be—eventually giving you an adrenalin rush of emotion called fear. When this connection takes place between the thought and the emotions it begins to fill your entire being and it becomes a living force. This seed of thought then energized by emotion will literally create the environment of fear and even terror. Anything that connects with our emotions becomes a very strong power.

The church has taught for years that emotions are not important. I say to you that your emotions and your thought life is the creative side of you. Your emotions are essential for everything to happen. Miracles are released through our emotions. Jesus was moved with compassion. Compassion released miracles—even the raising of the dead.

The power and Glory of God in the anointing are released through the gateway of human affection. This is why Paul stated to the church in Corinth that they were restricted in their affections (see 2 Cor. 6:12).

We have to feel what we do. When our thinking connects with the feeling of what we do, THE SEED IS PLANTED by desire! A power is released. It's the law of union where two things (or people) come into agreement.

> *When evil desire is conceived, it gives birth to sin, and sin when it is fully matured, brings forth death* (James 1:15).

When evil desire is conceived by lust (emotion) and thought, the two coming together form a creative power bond of agreement that brings forth (to breed or to create) sin. This phrase "bring forth" is the same as the plant that comes from the seed. It is the process of the Creation Law of Reproduction at work. Your thoughts manifest in the natural—like begets like.

THOUGHTS SHAPE OUR WORLD

Thoughts are living and powerful and when they connect with emotions they bring forth or create substance in our lives. Our thoughts become the gateway to the supernatural realm as desire mixes with the heart.

When I am meditating on the Word of God and revelation begins to flow in me and through me, my whole being seems to be flooded with light. And not only light, but flooded with the tranquil peace of the life of God. My emotions and the revelation that is coming from God's mind is being planted in the soil of my spirit-man. You know when God is speaking and your whole being is filled up with God!

Revelation is not just an abstract thought—it is connected with feeling that buries life deep inside us. And when this happens, a seed is planted. Conception has taken place. And with follow through, that revelation will bring to birth in our life.

This is the process of Creation! As a man thinks... so he will become!

THE HIDDEN POWER OF IMAGINATION

This New Glory Generation will move in the understanding and the wonderful release of the creative power of imagination. They will birth the will and purposes of God in the earth with mind-boggling authority over the elements in the physical realm. Jesus considered imagination as reality.

What you imagine in thought as it connects with your emotions will bring forth a birthing. Remember The Creation Law of Reproduction is irrevocable and unchangeable. What you plant will reproduce. It will come to pass. It will come forth!

SUPERNATURAL GATEWAYS OF DARKNESS

CAUTION: READER DISCRETION ADVISED

What you are about to read is the accurate account of details and activities that led to the death of Anton LaVey, who was the founder of the first church of Satan in Los Angeles, California. The reason I am including this section in this book is not to bring attention to, or glorify the occult in any way, shape, or form, but rather to show the inherent nature and creative design and capacity of mankind and the reality of those who practice moving as gateways of darkness. God has given us a beautiful gift called free will which is the ability to choose what we will do with the life He has given to us. For most reading this book we are glorious set free by the Blood of Jesus Christ and are after the deeper things of God by the Holy Spirit. Unfortunately, there are those who choose to live life for the wrong reason and some with full intent of promoting darkness with the deepest of intention. Each and every one of us is a gateway of the supernatural either by choice or default. What you are about to read is the account told by Dave Bryan,

Pastor of the Church of Glad Tidings in Yuba City, California. WARN-ING: This testimony will shock many! My hope is that it will impact you to pursue Jesus Christ to the fullest. Again, reader discretion is advised.

ANTON LAVEY – THE REAL STORY

The Calm Before the Storm
Dave Bryan, Pastor of the Church of Glad Tidings

ANTON LAVEY

I suppose it's safe to say that this story started in Nampa, Idaho in 1957—when I was born. I think that's how God weaves His tapestries in our lives; a strand here and a strand there— some of which may seem a bit out of place at the time, simply because our perspectives are so myopic ...so limited ...so lacking in the depth and contours of God's bigger purposes and plans for our futures. Anyway, whenever it started, the story DEFINITELY shifted into hyperspace in June of 1997. The catalyst be-hind what I now recognize as a radical makeo-ver of my spiritual world-view came with a phone call from Jack Schisler, an old missionary/prophet guy who had spent his entire adult life in evan-gelism and church planting efforts in Central and South America.

Jack was old; so old that we had already dubbed him, "the Ancient of Days." Even though that's a biblical title for God, it seemed to fit Jack well; not only because he was ancient, but also because he reminded us so much of God in other ways, too. He had been a friend and mentor to my father, Gail, who had been a Pentecostal pastor for most of his life. After my father died, Jack had been especially kind and fatherly to Cheryl and I, who were already busy pastoring The Church of Glad Tidings, in Yuba City, Cali-fornia. A full eight years earlier, in '89, Jack had called from his home in

Hemet, Southern California. He said that he had been praying, when the Spirit of God impressed on him to give me a book.

I arranged for Jack to visit GT (the common handle for the Church Of Glad Tidings), and he came with book in hand to deliver his message to us from the Holy Spirit. It was a simple message, and can still be found written in Jack's hand in the front cover of what I came to call "the book from the Twilight Zone." If it weren't for Jack's hand-written message, I'm sure I'd have thrown the whole book away, but – being from Jack, it was something of value to me as a keepsake. The message was this:

> *"To Dave & Cheryl, our dear friends that we love: May this true account equip you to take your rightful place in the front lines of spiritual warfare! Your friend, Jack Schisler."*

"What a sweet, ol' guy!" I thought to myself (totally over-looking the now obvious implications of the prophetic message he was delivering!) It didn't take long, though, for me to briefly peruse the book, and determine conclusively that the subject matter just wasn't for me. It was too weird, entirely!

I grew up as a country boy on a small ranch in Emmett, Idaho. We didn't even believe in weird, much less involve ourselves in it. Grandpa "Doc" Bryan used to always say, "Don't believe ANYTHING you hear, and only half of what you see!" As contrary as that is to authentic, biblical Christianity, it had a certain down-home country appeal to it that I found attractive, and I had for years prided myself in not being gullible or easily conned in any matters spiritual or otherwise. Part of this "can't be conned" M.O. of mine was a firm aversion to anything strange or "out of the box." The "Book from the Twilight Zone" more than qualified as both; so, committed to saving it as "memorabilia from people important to me" I decided to file it in my office library on my "Strange Books" shelf, where it set neglected for a full eight years before Jack finally let the prophetic hammer fall on me again.

I have intentionally omitted any complicity of my wife, Cheryl in this reluctance to explore the Spiritual "X" Files for a number of reasons. Firstly, it would be a terrible misrepresentation to do so, as she was waving the "Me! Me! Me! Pick Me!" flag from the very beginning; and had specifically asked to read "the book from the Twilight Zone" on a number of occasions during those eight years of "conscientious avoidance" on my part. Cheryl has always been more spiritually sensitive than me, and is a true spiritual adventurer. She seems to have a keen eye for the obvious in these things, where I historically haven't been able to "find my butt with both hands" in these matters. Anyway, as the granddaughter of famous '50's healing evangelist, A. A. Allen, she seems to have inherited a significant share of that mantle of "faith and power" that Grandpa Allen was so well known for. So, she was eager for action from the get-go!

That brings us to June of 1997, when Jack again called from somewhere south of the border with an urgent prophetic message for me – one that he insisted was too intense to communicate except in person. He did, however, remind me that EIGHT YEARS AGO he had delivered a message to me from the Holy Spirit concerning preparation for "front-line spiritual warfare!"

At the time of this 2nd commissioning, we were pastoring a fairly happy church of about 1,000 unsuspecting believers, and I held a respectable leadership position with a semi-charismatic, neo-denominational network of sorts whose leadership proudly viewed themselves as believing the whole Bible and living in the power of the anointing of Pentecost. As Mark Twain so aptly observed, "Our reputations greatly exceed us!" And so it was with me – a religiously educated and seemingly successful spiritual leader that knew virtually nothing about the reality of the spirit world, and tragically, had been fairly content to remain so.

Jack's follow-up message to me after my 8-year stint of dereliction of training duty was painfully simple and straightforward. He said:

"David, God's given you eight years to prepare for spiritual warfare

– which you have neglected and wasted. So now, you're about to be face-to-face with the devil, and you're not ready for it!"

"Gee, Jack! Just give it to me straight!" I thought to myself. "And, by the way, which part of that prophecy was supposed to be for "exhortation, edification or comfort?"

Within a few short days of that "prophetic jack-slappin'" all hell broke loose at GT. It was then that I really found myself longing for another leisurely 96-month window for training and preparation in "spiritual weapons and tactics." Instead, we were "up to our ears in alligators" – the Leviathan type – and none of us had any idea of what we were doing.

Jack's prophecy of being "face to face with the devil" broke like a storm the next week in an avalanche of such surreal, bizarre spiritual experiences that even now, all these years later, it's nearly overwhelming just recounting the ordeal. After being raised in the home of an Assembly of God pastor, graduating from Portland Bible College, pastoring a flourishing church, and serving on the Apostolic Leadership Team of Minister's Fellowship International, I found myself repenting of religion, and seriously seeking God in fasting and prayer to content with bigger-than-life, up close and personal, "in your face" demonstrations of demonic power that I didn't realize were even possible ...*anywhere* ...much less in Yuba City, California!

Although the demonic fire-storm we went through manifested in and through men, women and children of all classes and back-grounds from "raised-in-church Christians" to generational Satanists who were conceived in satanic rituals and dedicated to Satan from the womb. It all served the same purpose: To make real in our lives—AND THEIRS—the awesome reality of the Good News of Isaiah 61:1-3 and Luke 4:18-19!

During this season we learned and grew in our experiential knowledge of the demonic, the schemes of Satan, and how to overcome them. We saw well-mannered men and women, normally in their right mind, suddenly fall on the ground, contort their bodies, slither like snakes, claw, bite, and rage profanities in demonic voices. We thought this was the fulfillment of Jack's prophetic word about coming, "face-to-face with the devil." In reality this was just leading up to it!

THE GREAT WAR BEGINS

She seemed much like any other of the folks who came forward that next Sunday to commit their lives to Christ, and to receive His forgiveness and saving grace; maybe a bit more tentative, and obviously from a difficult background, but nothing that immediately tipped us off to who she was and where she had come from. She prayed the prayer for repentance and forgiveness with the others, and even came to the follow-up room after the service to receive the literature on *"The New Life"* and *"After Becoming a Christian, What's Next?"* She said her name was Ramona Jarnagin, and that the scars and braces on her face were from a recent accident. Curious as to her background, and sensing her uneasiness in a church setting, I asked if she understood the importance of repentance, and if she felt there was anything else she might need to specifically repent of. She looked sheepishly at the ground, and nervously tapped her left pointer finger to her lips, then hesitantly admitted that she had occasionally "sung karaoke" in bars and clubs before. "Well," I chuckled, "The blood of Jesus certainly has the power to wash all THAT away!" I gave her another little booklet entitled, "Your Church Family" and invited her to come to the meetings as often as possible.

Mondays were usually reserved for my day off but I had to stop by GT to take care of a few things. As we walked into the lobby and waved to Juanita, Cheryl's sister, she motioned to us from the front office, holding the phone up with one of those, "I think you'd better handle this one" looks in her eye. On the phone was a desperate woman who claimed that I had prayed with her the day before, and that her life was in danger by people who "were trying to kill her again." It was little "what's her name" who prayed to receive

Jesus and confessed to occasionally singing Karaoke in bars. Now she was crying, frantic, and her story had changed dramatically. She HADN'T been in an accident. Her face had been badly broken up by a recent murder attempt from satanic coven members that she had formerly been in league with. Now, the same satanic witches who had tried to kill her before were after her again, to complete the job. It all sounded a bit surreal, and besides, it was Monday; but when I offered to call the police for her, she begged me not to, and the phone went dead. Fortunately, she had already explained to Juanita where she was hiding, so Cheryl and I drove over to check things out. We found her hiding in the bushes near the courthouse, and fetched her from her hiding place. The next thing I knew, Cheryl had invited her home with us to live in our guest room!

"Hell Motel" - Yuba City, California

We spent the rest of the day moving her out of "Hell Motel" – as we learned to call it – and into our place with Cheryl and I and "the Three Amigos;" James, Josh and Joe. That whole relocation process took a grand total of about an hour, most of it spent on the commute. She didn't own a thing

that couldn't fit nicely into a few grocery bags. For anyone with a keen eye for the obvious, it was clear that she was "on the run." We felt deep compassion for her, and welcomed her into our home until she could get squared around again. As for the witches who were trying to kill her? ...well ...I'd been pastoring long enough to know that hard times and desperate circumstances could get a person at least "half a bubble out of plum" in their reasoning abilities, and could give rise to vain imaginations of all shapes and sizes. We've also always felt that the best medicine for most human emotional and spiritual ailments is sustained doses of God's love, so we weren't really too worried about the witches assassination agenda, or anything else she might have been "imagining" at the time. We put it in the same file as her Karaoke story, and figured we'd let God sort it out.

We moved her into the guest room upstairs, just across the hall from the boys' bedrooms, and went to sleep that night with the joy of heart that comes from helping those in need. Just a few hours later, we would be introduced to the demonic conjurings of "the Witching Hour" – which soon came to be our least favorite time of night.

Promptly at 2 AM we were awakened from a sound sleep by a God-awful curdling scream that flooded the whole house. Amidst the demonic shrieks and human cries for help, we heard Ramona's body come tumbling headlong down the first flight of stairs and crash into the wall of the landing with enough impact to shake the whole house. An instant later, she was thrown down the second flight of stairs and rolled up against our bedroom door, shrieking in sheer terror of what was happening to her! As we jumped out of bed, and scrambled to turn on the lights and "gird up our loins," it was obvious that the spiritual climate of our usually peaceful home had been invaded by gross evil. Before we were even able to open the door, we heard Joe, our youngest son (only eleven at the time) praying in the Holy Spirit and rebuking the devil! Later he would tell us that the Lord had awakened him before the incident began, and he was already praying when the spiritual fire-works erupted!

The Spirit World

The evil spirit that we confronted that first night was a powerful spirit of murder called "NAK" that Ramona was all too familiar with.   Amidst its curses, threats, and other-worldly howls, NAK managed to manipulate Ramona long enough to give us a message from "the dark side." The message got our attention, and served as a "heads up" that the fulfillment of Jack's prophecy had only just begun! NAK claimed a right to kill Ramona based on "spiritual alliances" that she had established by her past involvement in "conjurings," satanic rituals, dark covenants, oaths and pledges from her past.

As Cheryl & I and the boys gathered around the tormented woman at the bottom of the stairs that night, rebuking demons in Jesus' name and doing everything we could to keep the powerful spirit that called itself NAK from using her own hands, feet & teeth to harm or kill her or one of us, we knew that this mystery woman had been involved in something far more danger-ous and diabolical than "singing Karaoke" in a few bars. As we were soon to discover, this was just the first skirmish of "the great war."

In this brief overview, it's really not possible to do much more than briefly allude to a host of experiences and discoveries we made during the next tumultuous year. This amazing true story deserves a full-length book to recount the astonishing details. Suffice it to say here that Ramona a.k.a. ReyRey LaVey lived with us for eleven months, and the maturing process of working her through into "the glorious liberty of the children of God" (Rom. 8:21) is still underway! Soon after the NAK ATTACK, we discovered that our "house guest" was conceived in a sex ritual between Anton LaVey and an Illini Indian witch for the purpose of producing a "convergence" be-tween the dark powers of Illini Indian sorcery and Crowleyan "sex magic" of which the late Anton LaVey was to become one of the world's foremost authorities. As we began to confront the powers of hell and battle them for Rey Rey's soul, we also discovered the depths of Satanic Ritual Abuse to which she had been subjected all of her life, and the dark and forebod-ing plans that the Church of Satan had for her. More significant still, we experienced first-hand the awesome, raw power of Christ's redeeming love, and His unswerving commitment to "save to the uttermost" all that come to God through faith in Him" (Heb. 7:25). Rey Rey (who legally changed her name to DeborahJoy Bryan in order to disassociate with Anton LaVey and her unwanted roots in Satanism) became an official and permanent part of our family, and we love her dearly!

During the months preceding the death of Anton LaVey, DeborahJoy suf-fered incredibly at the hands of demonic powers, each of which made some claim to her based on Satanic Ritual alliances through which she had been "dedicated" to the Prince of Darkness. Never having an opportunity to choose otherwise, she had been groomed from the time of her conception to endure the Crowleyan "Rituals of Defilement" in preparation to become a Bride of Satan!" DeborahJoy had already suffered through six of these seven "Rituals of Defilement," leading up to the intended "Bride of Satan" ceremony that was scheduled for the night that Anton died! But God (and DeborahJoy) had other plans! Desperately wanting to avoid that horrendous fate, DeborahJoy (still "Rey Rey" at the time) had decided to escape from the Church of Satan, or to die trying; and apart from God's gracious intervention, she most certainly would have "died trying!" The Lord, however, had something entirely different in mind for her – glorious plans that "accompany salvation!" (Heb. 6:9).

It's difficult to even estimate how many hours of intense (often mind-boggling) spiritual conflict we slogged through from June until October of 1997. During these raging battles with dark forces, we discovered the pervasive reality of a powerful but unseen spirit world all around us, and learned how these evil cosmic forces desperately sought a "legal right" to operate through human-kind as "portals" from their realm to ours. We discovered that dark spirits (both demonic and human) could manipulate for their own use ANY physical bodies – human or animal – that were not protected by a spiritual power greater than their own! During those days, (and often since) we witnessed men, women, children, animals and even inanimate objects (like computers, automobiles, electrical lighting systems, and stereos) manipulated by dark spiritual forces of both demonic and human origin in order to accomplish their nefarious purposes. We discovered that *many* of the inexplicable and sometimes bizarre actions of unwitting people were the direct result of their physical body being hijacked by a spiritual entity (human, demonic or angelic) that - much like a thug in a car-jacking – simply forced the rightful "driver" into the passenger seat in order to temporarily take control to use the vehicle (their body) for another purpose. In such cases, very often the victim of the "body-jacking" has no more awareness of what is transpiring than Balaam's famous donkey had of her conversation with the greedy prophet.

From the day the Great War broke upon as, day-by-day and hour-by-hour we experienced all things weird and wonderful. All of our beautiful theories about what was and wasn't possible, were murdered by a gang of ugly facts! We began to take at face value what Scripture states as a bold fact: "*All things are possible...*" (Matt. 19:26; Mark 10:27; Mark 14:36). We discovered that evil spirits were "legalists" who skillfully take advantage of every area in our lives where we have ever "given place to the devil!" (see Eph. 4:27). We discovered, too, that they are aggressive and persistent in their claims against us, and will ALWAYS exert themselves to take as much control in any human life (Christian or not) as that individual will yield to them, either by complicity with evil or by ignorance, intimidation and deception. We also saw vividly demonstrated to us the importance of heeding the warning of Scripture to "be fully aware of our adversaries' evil strategies" (2 Cor. 2:11).

I can't help but chuckle now, as I think back over my religious and spiritual education, and muse over how ill-equipped it left me in regard to understanding and participating effectively in the realm of spiritual reality. I had graduated with honors from a reputable Bible college, having earned an "A" in the offered classes on angelology and demonology; and yet I knew virtually NOTHING about either camp! I'll never forget DeborahJoy's observation one day as she woefully concluded, "Gee Dad... for a spiritual leader, you don't know much about spirits, do you?" As embarrassing as it was to admit, I knew she was absolutely right!

THE GREAT SPIRITUAL SHOW DOWN AT THE "NOT SO OK CORRAL"

Those five months leading up to Halloween Eve of 1997 were so filled with spiritual phenomena and sensational happenings that it's not possible to even mention most of those amazing events in a cursory account of this nature. It is, however, important to recognize a small team of real spiritual heroes without whose help we simply would have been overwhelmed. These stalwart spiritual warriors were willing to risk everything to stand with us in a life and death struggle against the hords of hell in order to rescue DeborahJoy from the dark designs that the Black Pope (Anton) and the Church of Satan had for her. At the top of this list is Cheryl's sister Juanita and her husband Duane "Big Dog" Talbott. They nearly lived with us during those months, along with Jill "Kimi Bear" Underhill. Eric Kruegar and a handful of other "spiritual rangers" help pray us through those dark nights at the height of the intensity of The Great War. Lastly, our precious sons, James, Josh & Joe were both courageous and cooperative during the entire "bruhah-hah" – though not always excited about the nightly "exorcism" and extreme negative spiritual climate it often brought into the home.

In order to understand just what happened that Halloween Eve, and how Anton LaVey died that night it's important to understand at least the basics regarding the interaction of spirits on what is often referred to today as the "astral plane." Jesus taught in the Gospels that evil spirits coveted bodies of flesh to express themselves through. Physical bodies become "portals" of sorts for inter-dimensional entities to express themselves on the physical plane that we view as "natural" or "normal." Jesus taught that disembodied, evil spirits would continue to search for expression in the human realm until they found a physical body through which they could express themselves. In much the same way, occult adepts (and many others) can "leave" their own bodies and travel on this "astral plane" to "hi-jack" the body of another human being, or even an animal. They commandeer this physical body by force, in much the same way that a thug may force his way into someone else's automobile while the driver is stopped at a traffic light. Even though the vehicle does not rightfully belong to him, the thug forces the rightful driver out of the driver's seat and asserts control. In very similar manner, "spirits" – whether angelic, demonic or human – are able to pull off a "body-jacking" in order to use that body as a vehicle of expression or action in keeping with their specific agenda. In the case of a human spirit perpetrating the "take-over" of another physical host body, they remain remotely attached to their own human bodies through an ethereal "silver cord" of life. This enables them to "return" to their own bodies after they've finished using the high-jacked body for their intended purposes. Understanding this is essential in order to realize what really happened that Halloween Eve to Anton LaVey, and to recognize the power of intercessory prayer to thwart the plans of evil and rescue DeborahJoy from otherwise certain death.

From the time that DeborahJoy moved into our home and we experienced that first "NAK Attack," the game was on with Anton and his Church of Satan cronies. The conflict was a simple one. Anton had plans for ReyRey to be a contender for the Bride of Satan, and God had plans for Deborah-Joy to be a part of the Bride of Christ! Neither party was willing to negotiate, so a power encounter was inevitable from the get-go! Early on in the conflict we began to have visitors (including Anton himself) come to our home and church property in the middle of the night to leave amulets, cursed corn, fetishes and the carcasses of sacrifices animals on our property. Bizarre messages were left on the answering machines both at home and at the church office, threatening to burn us out; or more threatening still, to rape, torture or murder us if we continued to interfere with their plans. Armed with a simple faith in Christ's omnipotence, and His great love for His children, we continued on, undaunted by the threats. When "second-hand" messages weren't having their desired effect on us, Anton began to over-power DeborahJoy and speak and act directly through her, in the fashion described above. Due to the many years of Satanic Ritual Abuse that DeborahJoy had suffered through, there were many points of vulnerability through which she could still be overpowered and manipulated by Anton. Knowing every weakness, every secret of the past, every ritual involvement, every implanted fetish, he exploited her in every way he could, trying desperately to intimidate her and convince her that any hope of lasting freedom and a new life in Christ was "too little, too late."

It was during these intense encounters with Anton that he would communicate to us his disdain for Christ and all that Christ represented. In turn, we would communicate to him the futility of fighting against the Spirit of the Almighty God, and attempted to share with him the truth of God's saving grace which was now so evidently at work in DeborahJoy's heart and soul. Because of Anton's perversity and defiling language, we soon learned to circumvent his ability to speak through DeborahJoy's physical body by literally "stuffing a sock" in her mouth to muffle his threats and blasphemies, each time he staged an appearance by "hi-jacking" her physical faculties of speech, thought and volition. We soon learned to restrain DeborahJoy's body as carefully as possible so as not to "hurt the host" while we muffled Anton's ranting. Then we would read God's Word to him until he wearied of the spiritual pummeling, after which he would leave abruptly and defiantly, following the Silver Cord to return "home" to His own body. Because this happened so frequently in those days, it afforded me the rare opportunity to explain the Good News of Christ's redeeming love and saving grace to Anton LaVey before his death, perhaps more thoroughly and clearly than he had ever heard it before. The night of his death I was reminded of how often he had heard of Christ's loving offer of salvation, not just to DeborahJoy, but to him personally, and had hardened his heart and refused God's gracious offer of salvation! Looking back, I'm very grateful for that opportunity.

Too often Christians engaged in spiritual warfare begin to think of those involved in occult activities as "the enemy" instead of seeing them as prisoners of war who have been "taken captive by the devil to do his will." Little did we know at the time that we would see the sober warning of Proverbs 29:1 realized in a surprisingly dramatic way that Halloween Eve as Anton "space of repentance" suddenly expired. The warning couldn't be stated more succinctly:

> *"Anyone who refuses to repent after being warned many times will one day be suddenly destroyed without another chance!"*

During our skirmishes with Anton and his coven cronies, though, our minds weren't on divine judgment, but upon divine mercy and God's gracious offer of salvation promised to anyone who was willing to acknowledge Him as Lord and Savior. DeborahJoy WAS willing and we were determined to stand with her – come hell or high water – until she was free from the terrible chains of her past abuse. Often we found ourselves praying for other member of her former satanic coven, as well, and hoping that they would follow DeborahJoy's example, and allow the Lord to translate them out of the Kingdom of Darkness and into the Kingdom of God's love, life, light and glorious liberty!

Anton had, during our frequent exchanges, adopted the habit of calling me "Preacher Boy," and of reminding me that I was no match for him in the realm of spiritual phenomena. He often reminded me that he was a world-class sorcerer, and that I was a virtual "nobody" who served a weakling savior. He saw Christ as a loser, who died in humiliation on a cross because He was too weak to defend Himself against the Dark Lord, Satan. To Anton, the Gospel account of the resurrection of Christ was a pathetic attempt of His followers to "save face" after the humiliating defeat of Christ's crucifixion. Anton had boasted all along that when the time for the Halloween Rituals came that we would see whose god was the most powerful, Satan or Christ.

He also openly claimed that during the up-coming Bride of Satan ceremony scheduled for Halloween morning that his daughter (Rey Rey / DeborahJoy) WOULD be present, either as "the Bride of Satan" or as a blood sacrifice to him. He often taunted us with this horrific scenario, claiming that if our influence caused DeborahJoy to refuse to be Satan's bride, that her blood would be on our hands, not his! He seemed to exude confidence that they would be able to apprehend DeborahJoy when the time came, and to do with her whatever they pleased.

By then, it was obvious to us that Anton had significant demonic powers, and that no amount of "natural" precautionary measures could keep him away. Our confidence, though, was in Christ alone, not in human ingenuity or even in spiritual gifts bestowed by the Holy Spirit to help us in the fray. During these dark months of spiritual conflicts we encountered scores of evil spirits claiming the right to DeborahJoy's soul based on everything from implanted fetishes, blood rituals, coven oaths and conjurings, bloodline inheritance, and soul ties based on sex rituals and the like. Despite Anton's frequent rantings and the unrelenting assault of the demons day and night, we kept our hopes bright by contemplating the "great and precious promises" of Scripture and frequently reminiscing on the indefatigable, never failing, unconquerable love of God that NOTHING (including demons) can separate us from! The comforting words from Romans chapter eight were like a strong tower of refuge during those days (see Rom. 8:31-39). Those precious words ministered new life, strength, courage and resolve to us over and over and over again.

As Halloween Eve of that year approached, a small group of us fasted and prayed for the strategy of heaven to combat the nefarious plans of Anton LaVey, Leviathan, and their underlings in the Church of Satan regarding DeborahJoy. We knew they fully anticipated success, albeit without good reason. Simple logic from an unbiased observer would undoubtedly look toward a different outcome resulting from a spiritual power encounter between the two kingdoms, solely based on the fact of God's recurring interventions in any and all of the cults previous attempts to abduct her. I raised this point one night to Anton, as he once again "hi-jacked" DeborahJoy's body and managed to punch me in the face before anyone realized what was going on. As he laughed at me, mocked Christ and demeaned me as the stupid "Preacher Boy" who had no spiritual prowess and was no match for his amassed powers as a black sorcerer, I asked what to me was a glaringly obvious question:

"Anton, if you have such great power, and we have so little – as you often boast – then what's keeping you from taking DeborahJoy from us? Why not just sweep her away from us now with your vast, supernatural powers, and be done with it?" I asked. Though his answer was obviously accurate, it was also quite apparent that he had failed to think through its undeniable implications. His answer...

"You're nothing, Preacher Boy! I'd destroy you in an instant if it weren't for those damned angels all around you!" All it took that night to make Anton leave in a fit of rage was a simple and obvious response:

'In other words, Anton, you would LOVE to destroy us, and abduct DeborahJoy, but YOU JUST CAN'T SEEM TO GET 'ER DONE because of the continual intervention of the hosts of heaven, that surround and protect us, RIGHT?!"

We all knew it to be true! Many times we had seen the Hosts of Heaven miraculously intervene to protect us from danger and from certain death.

Anton and company had made it very plain that Halloween Eve would be the scheduled showdown, so our team was prayed up and most of us had been fasting (again!). We figured they would plan some sort of a power play to abduct DeborahJoy that evening just before the scheduled Bride of Satan ceremony during the Witching Hour beginning at midnight as October 30th transitioned into the 31st. For a counter-offensive we had planned to meet at our place with our SWAT (Spiritual Weapons And Tactics) Team at 9:00 PM on the 30th, and to have a 3-hour stint of robust prayer and intercession to preempt whatever they had planned. Knowing they were desperate, and having been already threatened repeatedly injury and death, we were prepared both naturally and spiritually for "whatever" they planned to bring to the fight. We had also alerted close family and friends both locally and abroad to pray with us that night, and were later to learn that the Holy Spirit had specifically stirred up other intercessors and spiritual warriors who were prompted to pray specifically against the evil strategies of the Church of Satan that same night.

Cheryl and I were keeping a close eye on Deborah, and "Big Dog," Juanita, "Kimi Bear" (Jill Underhill) and Ernie (Eric Krueger) had all tried to get some sleep in preparation of the inevitable "shoot out at the OK Corral" that we were all anticipating that night. Just 30 minutes or so before the team was scheduled to begin arriving, Deborah Joy came down the stairs from her room and announced cheerily that she was going to walk down the street to the 7/11 to get some coffee before the action started for the night.

"Say WHAT?" I asked her. Reminding her that there was a "winner takes all" showdown underway, and that her very life was at stake in it, I sent her back up to her room to pray, but instantly told Cheryl that something "wasn't right" with DeborahJoy. We KNEW she would NEVER had made that suggestion on her own that night. Being there alone with her in a very big, old Victorian house, I asked Cheryl to guard the back door and holler if DeborahJoy tried to leave the house that way, while I positioned myself on the porch watching the front door.

Two police cars suddenly screeched into our drive-way with lights and sirens on. As I stood to inquire why they were there, to my shock and horror DeborahJoy came bursting through our front door... with Anton in "full control" of all of her faculties! She rushed wildly past me, screaming for the police to help "rescue" her from us. "Kidnappers! Abusive! They've been holding me as a prisoner here, trying to brain-wash me with all their religious shit!" she screamed (in that low, raspy voice that I had come to recognize from Anton's "body-jacking" episodes)! She ran like a terrified, abused child across the yard toward the officers. Naturally, I jumped up and ran to catch her, and was very nearly shot in the process. The Yuba City police officers "pulled down" on me, and ordered me firmly back to the porch, as they showed DeborahJoy to the safety of one of their squad cars.

The attending policemen, now joined by a third squad car and fourth officer, sternly announced that they were responding to a "911" emergency call from our residence by a Deborah Bryan, who stated that she had been kidnapped and held against her will for months by a dangerous religious fanatic that was trying to force her to become one of his followers! As I tried desperately to reason with them, I couldn't help admire the diabolical scheme that had been contrived. There was simply no natural defense against it! As I blubbered about DeborahJoy not being "in her right mind" they countered by asking if I was a licensed psychologist or medical doctor, and went quickly on to remind me that – even if I was – it wasn't legal to detain another adult against their will. "It's what we call 'kidnapping,' Mr. Bryan, and it's a very serious criminal offense!" they said, as they ordered me to a sitting position on the front porch step.

As they "huddled" to determine whether or not to immediately arrest me, I quickly called a co-worker and very close friend, Lou Bininger. Lou and I had worked closely together for a decade on the pastoral leadership team of the Church of Glad Tidings. His official job description for GT was to serve as "Community Liaison" for the church, helping to fulfill our ministry motto to "Find a Need and Meet It, & Find a Hurt and Heal It" in our bi-county area. Louie's simply "the best" at what he does, and most of the area emergency responders know him as a "Community Service" guy who oversees several chaplaincy programs, helps single moms, parolees and juvenile delinquents, and heads up the bi-county Trauma Intervention Program. As such, he's a "frequent flier" at crime scenes, accidents and any other traumatic happenings about town. Most emergency responders aren't even aware that he has an office at the church, and that's the way we've intentionally kept it. So, I called Lou and asked him to get here ASAP!

Fortunately for all the "good guys" the officers were in a bit of a quandary as to how best to handle the situation. They were sure about what to do with DeborahJoy. They would escort her away from the premises to wherever she wanted to go! But there was anything but consensus over what to do with "the Pastor!" One of the officers attended Glad Tidings. Like most of the church attendees at the time, he had no idea who DeborahJoy was, or what danger she was in. As I tried to explain the danger she was in, it suddenly sounded bizarre even to me! How was I to explain to rationalistic, western-minded law enforcement officers who are TRAINED to be skeptical that DeborahJoy was not actually in control of her own body, or that the voice raging out of her? How could I possibly convince them that Cheryl and I had lovingly protected DeborahJoy for the past 5 months, and mercifully guarded her from the sinister plans of the Church of Satan? Had it all been in vain? Had the satanic sorcerer finally won the war?

Finally, Lou showed up. Praise God! Maybe all wasn't lost! Naturally, they welcomed Lou's professional help as a respected trauma counselor, and allowed him to speak to me. I tried to give him the skinny in a brief and amazing overview of what was transpiring. As one of my closest friends and a co-pastor with me at GT, naturally Lou knew some of the story, but we only had precious seconds to forge a plan. I was about to be arrested for felony kidnapping and who knows what all else, and DeborahJoy was about to be led away to her horrific demise and the hands of a group of frenzied Satan worshippers. While Lou, Cheryl and I breathed a desperate prayer for God's help and the officers debated whether or not there was a recourse other than arresting me on the spot that night, Anton sat in the back of a squad car, scoffing at us with triumphant disdain, and flipping us off with both hands. We could hear him laughing out loud as he mocked the idiocy of the Preacher Boy and the impotence of the Preacher Boys "pathetic God."

In a flash of thought that was definitely "smarter than me" I slipped Cheryl's cell phone into Lou's hand and said, "Lou, it's imperative that you slip this phone into DeborahJoy's jacket pocket without Anton knowing it, and that you SOMEHOW convince the police to NOT take me to jail tonight." "I'll do my best," Lou said. And anyone that knows Lou Bininger knows that "his best" is a heck of a lot!

Anton was more than a little surprised when Lou suddenly swung the squad car door open and slid in next to him? Her? Anyway, Lou took one for the team that night as Anton raged and sworn and pummeled him with DeborahJoy's little fists and feet. To any bystander with "a keen eye for the obvious" it was immediately clear that Lou's presence in the squad car was CAUSING trauma, not alleviating it! The officers rushed to pull him out before there was any serious blood-letting. Cool-head Lou ended the drama by his succinct professional evaluation: "Deborah Joy was DEFINITELY having a traumatic night, but she did, after all, have a long mental health history, and her accusations may all be a figment of her troubled imagination."

"Meanwhile," said the wise counselor, "Pastor Bryan is well respected in the community, and certainly posed no threat to anyone if allowed to remain at home until the accusations could be sorted through with more certainty." The Holy Spirit "did His thing" and suddenly, everybody agreed that Lou's assessment was a wonderful solution to an otherwise messy situation.

I was STERNLY lectured regarding the seriousness of the charges leveled against me by DeborahJoy, and forbidden to follow her or search for her that night. They would not disclose where they would drop her, simply saying they would be willing to take her anywhere she thinks she needs to go tonight, within reasonable driving limits. We had an understanding.

As Lou stood with me and Cheryl on our porch, the officers escorted DeborahJoy's body away into the dark of the night toward her satanic executioners, with Anton's spirit still smugly in control as he triumphantly waved to us a double-fisted version of the "screw you" salute through the back window of the squad car. If we had ever for even an instant mistakenly relied in any way on our own wisdom or ingenuity in the spiritual war that was raging for DeborahJoy's soul, it was painfully clear to us all in that unforgettable moment that — apart from the sovereign wisdom and intervening power of God, DeborahJoy's life would be snuffed out, and we would have to console ourselves in the fact that her many sins had been forgiven, and that her name was written in the Lamb's Book of Life. Her misery would finally be over, and her eternal reward would be enjoying the pleasures of Christ's presence, age without end.

Still... it just wasn't right!

As we paced the floors and cried out to the Lord, I knew I couldn't stand by and allow DeborahJoy's blood to be shed in a sacrifice to the powers of evil that night. I simply couldn't live with that. A strong anointing came over me. It may sound a bit "bigger than life," but that's just the way it happened. I told Lou and Cheryl to go in Lou's car to "Hell Motel" and watch for any suspicious happenings. Anton often drove around with his satanist cronies in a big black limousine, so we were all keeping an eye out for that. Somewhere, we figured that they had a rendezvous location. There, in all probability, members of the cult would be gathered around the High Priest's lifeless body, awaiting Anton's return from his nefarious "body-snatching" antics on the astral plane. This he wouldn't be able to do until DeborahJoy's body was in the custody of members of the coven, who could then subdue her and abduct her to "the Ranch" in the foothills near Grass Valley, some 40 miles away. Hmmm.... We needed some SERIOUS divine intervention!

As Lou and Cheryl headed for Hell Motel, I went a bit "Old Testament!" I strapped on my Kimber 1911 .45 and holstered a Glock .45 with several high capacity magazines. If DeborahJoy was going to die at the hands of wicked men that night, I had decided she wouldn't die alone. I headed out of town toward The Ranch scanning every shadow for the black limousine, and seriously hoping that God had a better idea. Thankfully, He did!

I was still on the outskirts of Marysville when I remembered the phone Lou had slipped in DeborahJoy's jacket pocket. I quickly dialed Cheryl's number, despite the risk of imprisonment if the officers choose to call me on it. They had forbidden me to attempt any further contact with DeborahJoy that night. Still, it was technically my wife's phone I was dialing. I decided it was worth the risk!

THE DEATH OF THE DARK POPE

Even if I live to be 1,000 years old, I'll never forget the brief exchange that followed, or the overwhelming sense of divine impetus that came over me simultaneously. Before any words were exchanged, I recognized Anton's malevolent laugh. He was gloating in pride, and seething with contempt for Christ and any who would seek to honor Him. I can easily imagine it was the same blind arrogance that caused his dark master to boast of his clever scheme to crucify Christ 2,000 years ago! He seemed to be intoxicated with pride and a false sense of satanic superiority as he cursed me in utter disdain, and mocked and blasphemed Christ Jesus, calling Him a pathetic weakling, and a fool! Then Anton exulted, "We'll drink Deborah-Joy's blood tonight in a ritual in honor of Satan! Where's the power of your pathetic Christ now, Preacher Boy?! You lose, just like I said you would!"

The Black Pope was still laughing as the phone went dead; but as the phone went dead in my hand, something far more powerful came alive in my heart! I suddenly was overcome with a knowledge that came from God. This was just like the crucifixion scenario! Christ allowed Satan to imagine he had won, and then, when he least expected it, dramatically turned the tables on him in an excruciating defeat that the Almighty had carefully engineered all along!

As I was praying for God's specific direction, my cell phone rang. It was Lou, who had staged himself in the shadows near the infamous "Hell Motel," and had just seen Deborah cross the street and enter the front door of the building, still moving sluggishly, as if in a trance. I was still only minutes away! As I spun my car around and headed back into town, I quickly called Jill, who by that time was at our house and was keeping the team updated as to what was going on.

The strategy came "clear and simple!" Anton was planning to take DeborahJoy's life, but she was still in town, right under our noses, and he was still "tip-toeing through the tulips" in the astral plane. We had the team focus in agreement on one prayer petition! Anton had done much more than harassed, mocked and threatened us! He planned DeborahJoy's murder, and had blasphemed Christ! We simply asked God for DeborahJoy's life in exchange for Anton's and petitioned the Lord to "sever the silver cord." Within a few quick minutes I had stopped my car in the road in front of Hell Motel. Lou and Cheryl were already in position, interceding and watching the back exit of the building. As I stood there in the road that night with the engine running and the door open, hands and heart lifted to heaven, I joined my faith with the others praying for God to intervene to do what needed done. Suddenly, the front doors burst open, and DeborahJoy came dashing out into my arms! "Help me, Daddy!" she screamed. She was back in control, with no spiritual hitch-hikers or high-jackers aboard.

DeborahJoy and I were in the car and out of the neighborhood in a hot second; Lou and Cheryl right behind us. It all happened so fast that there wasn't time to compare notes. We just leapt in the car and saturated the neighborhood with our sudden absence. On the way back across the river from Marysville to Yuba City, we were talking a million miles a minute, Deborah didn't remember a thing from the time of prayer we had with her in the front room that evening about 8:00 PM until she suddenly came back to her conscious awareness in an upstairs room in "Hell Motel." She was terrified! Things were frantic! The atmosphere was charged with the oppressive, stifling evil that is always attendant in a gathering of witches, warlocks and dark sorcerers. But there was something else pervading the gathering. There was massive confusion, mixed with anger and stark terror. Something had gone terribly wrong! The High Priest had "bounced!" The coven members and hierarchy of the Church of Satan were gathered around Anton's body, frantically reciting mantras, invoking power demons and attempting to pool their dark powers in a convergence that would somehow enable their High Priest to re-enter his physical body and resume his responsibilities in the important affairs of the evening. In all the confusion and frantic attempts to save the Black Pope, they hadn't even noticed when DeborahJoy came back to her senses, recognized where she was, and dashed out the apartment door, down the steps and out into the street! Thank God no one came after her. I was, after all, still "armed and dangerous!"

Soon after we were home behind locked doors and in the relative safety of our front room praising and worshipping the Lord for His mercies to DeborahJoy, she was suddenly overcome by a spirit so powerful and so perverse that its manifestation brought a sudden change in the entire atmosphere of our home! DeborahJoy's eyes bulged, elliptical and fiery red. The spirit that spoke through her lamented that we had killed the High Priest! Other than Deborah's brief assessment of the frantic happenings in the upper room of Hell Motel, this was the first confirmation that we had of what had actually transpired. The spirit identified itself as Leviathan, Anton LaVey's "power spirit" who was angered by Anton's unexpected, and his own sudden need for reassignment in a human accomplice or partner in evil. His appearance was very brief, but his message very clear. Anton was dead!

Minutes later, Deborah's still-vulnerable soul was high-jacked by another spirit, this one bewailing the passing of Anton by directly and specifically denouncing us as "murderers" for killing her father! The specifics of the accusation narrowed down the possible sources to Zeena or Karla. A quick inquiry indentified the "spiritual high-jacker" to be Zeena, to which we responded that we had implored the Lord to severe Anton's silver cord in order to rescue DeborahJoy, and that since she, too, was trespassing on the astral plane that she was in grave danger of the same! Realizing the imminent threat, she instantly left, and has not to our knowledge ever attempted a body-jacking maneuver of that sort against DeborahJoy from that day to this.

We spent the rest of that unforgettable morning of October 31st, 1997, worshipping Jesus, and reveling in His great mercy and grace to those who love Him. The months following that were filled with hours of mentoring DeborahJoy, and praying for the healing of her broken heart, and the renewing of her mind. All these years later, we are honored that she still calls us Dad & "Sissy" (her nick-name for Cheryl, who is just two days older than her) and considers herself a permanent part of the Bryan family. She is happily married to Billy Goodnight, who is our dear friend, and a part of the family now too! They live here in the Yuba City area, and are serving God together and attending the Church of Glad Tidings. Her daughter, Neecy, is also happily married, and raising a Christian family north of us in the Redding area. Their entire story remains one of the greatest testimonies of God's amazing grace and prevailing love that I have ever heard of! We continue to share the valuable lessons that we learned during those days with thousands of inquirers in this country and abroad through our Isaiah 61 Deliverance Conferences, School of Deliverance, and Tearing Down Stronghold's materials and seminars. While we remain grateful for all we learned during "The Great War!" we remain anxious to become ever more knowledgeable, and effective in helping people escape from the prison houses of spiritual torment and bondage, and experiencing ever-increasing realms of "the glorious liberty of the children of God!"

Real Life Account
Dave Bryan, Pastor of Glad Tidings Church Yuba City California

DAVE & CHERYL BRYAN

To the stories recounted above we could add many others. Instances of corporal bodies being pulled through physical structures, as was the case when evil spirits "pulled" Deborah's legs through the firewall of our Chevy van all the way up to her knees, yet when we rebuked them in Jesus' name, Deborah was miraculously pulled back into her seat with NO HARM done to either her legs or to the firewall of our van! Deborah's legs went through the firewall (area below dash, above the floorboard) of the van. She was being physically pulled against her will into the spirit world. She was screaming, "I am a natural person and you can not do this to me" all the while she was disappearing through the floorboard of the van... finally it broke and she returned to the original position in her car seat. Of course I was rebuking hell and praying in tongues frantically.

These stories are never questioned in many of the nations of the world who hold a more spiritual world-view than the "enlightened" nations of the West, where the great majority of the pastors and spiritual leaders criticize them as sensational and unreasonable. While we "amen" the stories of Jesus walking on the water or passing through the walls of buildings while in fully-physical form after His resurrection, why are we so quick to say, "That's impossible!" at the hearing of similarly miraculous accounts today? These clear examples of the "higher laws" of the spirit world should pave the way for any honest mind to admit to the reality of spiritually transcended physics being an expected reality in our day. Once there, the details are just that... DETAILS! Yet despite the frequent biblical examples of transcended physics, the traditions of western Christendom have been distorted by unabashed skepticism and a pervasive reliance on a rationalistic world view to the point that such accounts are nearly always written off – even by "Bible believing spiritual leaders" – as somewhere between fanciful imagination and blatant heresy. And because the church has largely relegated itself to the status of the "unbelievers" in this transcendent realm, many spiritually famished souls have found higher experiences in the dark realms of the occult.

What you've just read is a real life account. I did not "dummy this up" for the sake of the readers of this book. We live in a supernatural world, which is both good and evil, light and dark. The western world has subjugated its authority in the realm of the spirit to the devil because we flat refuse to accept anything we cannot wrap our small western mindset around. We have been taught that if we can't see it or touch it, it doesn't exist. This must change! It's time to get real. The world has been running to the occult because the church had not rightly represented God. The good news is that there is a generation arising that understands its position in Christ, and is not afraid to move in it. It's time for the real church of Jesus Christ to rise and shine for our Light has come.

Note:
Author: David El-Cana Bryan; 2011[21]

Questions and/or concerns regarding this amazing true story can be directed to me and Cheryl at: info@ChurchOfGladTidings.com

Chapter 6

ANOINTING, LIGHT & CREATIVE POWER

I'm sure the previous chapter was a stretch for many. However, the reality of the supernatural world is real regardless of what most of the church chooses to believe. The Lord is preparing a people, an army of God that will move with clear revelation and purpose in this generation—a people that will move in the light of His love in the last days. If you desire to be one of these, then you must abide in, walk in, and bear the fruit of love for personal transformation. When love flows from you, it is transformed into a power of light. When love turns into light and the light passes through you, you will experience the healing and transformation of that power— the light of God will charge through every atom of your being because love becomes a fantastic power of light. Supernatural light is healing, revelation, knowledge, understanding, and insight that flow from your mind and your lips as love and light.

JESUS AND THE DANCING GLORY

During another series of meetings held at the Transformation Center Church International with my good friend Andrey Shapovalov, it became clear to all that a new level of Glory was being offered to the church and the expectation was high. On first night of the event during worship, I saw the Lord enter the room dancing. He was spinning and twirling around the room and it was clear that He was happy. As I watched Him dance around the room He approached me and leaned into me grinning from ear to ear. He said, *"Jeff, I'm dancing with my brothers and sisters!"* I watched as He went from one person to the another and leaned into them. Then, as if to show me something new, the Lord approached me again. This time, as He leaned into me I saw on the front of His robe a golden menorah burning with seven flames. These flames were not orange in appearance, but were burning with the seven colors of the rainbow. Jesus smiled at me and danced off through the crowd. I knew exactly what He was showing me.

THE MENORAH AND THE SEVEN SPIRITS OF GOD

The Seven Spirits of God are the *Sevenfold Radiations of the Spirit* in Zechariah 3. Radiation is light and there are seven spectrums of light that we know of in the natural. The Lord was showing me these "Seven Radiations" of the Menorah were actually the Seven Spirits of God or the Seven Colors, Anointings, Angels, and Spirits burning before the throne of God. Jesus was dancing in the room with all Seven Spirits burning in His chest as the firstborn of a family of burning ones. As we are born again and filled with the Holy Spirit, there are actually levels of light or revelation in which we grow. We must be baptized in the Holy Ghost and Fire in order to burn with the Seven Flames. I want to add that these Seven Flames or Spirits of God are more than just anointings. They are indeed the Holy Spirit of God.

The following is a vision that was given to Lana that will help define what we are talking about here.

Lana's Vision with the 6.3-Karat Stone

In the meeting at Transformation Center, Seattle on the last night, Lana was caught up into a vision and saw a bright cloud that had come down

into the room in the appearance of a spiral or a whirlwind that was spinning very fast. As it was spinning, people were caught up into this cloud and would become completely transparent. Lana could see a menorah burning on the inside of each of the people. Then a second cloud whirled into the room and entered into the people and the burning lights on the menorah would come alive inside of them. In the meeting we began to shout "Grace! Grace!" from Zechariah 4 and God said, *"Now is the time that I will release through my Body, a Glory in the earth that has never been seen. For my Body will burn with the Seven Spirits together in unity and revival will sweep across the nations."*

The Lord said that we should not keep what we have to ourselves, but give it away. In the vision, angels came down in the meeting and placed a seal on the foreheads of the ones that were burning with the Seven Spirits of God. The angels said, "These are the Overcomers." When the angels would place a seal on the people, explosions would be released all over the earth. The more the seals were placed upon the people's foreheads, the more explosions would happen. The Lord was showing that in the Glory realm, not only one flame would burn as it did in previous anointings or levels, but in this season of the *new level*, all Seven flames must burn together. Only then would Revival go Global.

SEVEN SPIRITS BURNING

The Seven Sprits of God, according to Zechariah 3 and 4 are the *Seven Spirits burning before the Throne of God*. In Isaiah 11:2 they are the *Seven Spirits of the Lord*. In Revelation they are greeted by the *Seven Spirits* and are the *Seven Angels* (Messengers) In 2 Chronicles, they are the *Eyes of the Lord* that roam throughout the earth.

In the natural, we understand that there are seven spectrums of light and that these lights are represented in the color of the rainbow. They are - Red, Orange, Yellow, Green, Blue, Indigo and Purple. When put together these seven colors make up white light. In the book of Zechariah it says that the Seven Spirits of God are the *"Seven-fold Radiations of God"* (Zech. 3:9).

Radiation is light. These "Radiations" are colors that can be identified in the realm of the Spirit. Now there is natural light and heavenly light. These Seven colors work in tandem with each other in the natural. If you place the seven colors of the rainbow upright on the menorah, a mystery is revealed. Here you can see how these Seven colors and anointings work together in connection with one another with the Middle Green flame being the center shaft of the Menorah called *"The Spirit of the Lord shall Rest upon"* in Isaiah 11:2. This can also be found in Isaiah 61:1 and Luke 4:18 where Jesus spoke: *The Spirit of the Lord God rests upon Me, because He has anointed me to Preach.*

The Spirit of the Lord is the green Center color in the rainbow and the Center Shaft of the Menorah that all the other colors and flames flow from. The Spirit of Wisdom (Red) and the Spirit of Understanding (Purple) flow together as Wisdom and Revelation. The Spirit of Counsel (Orange) and the Spirit of Might (Indigo) flow together as instruction and power. The Spirit of Knowledge (Yellow) and the Spirit of the Fear of the Lord (Blue) flow together as the Fear of the Lord being the beginning of Knowledge. Let me explain further.

BUILDING FROM A HEAVENLY BLUEPRINT

Exodus 25:31-39 examines God's heavenly pattern for the lamp stand in Moses' tabernacle:

You shall also make a lamp stand of pure gold; the lamp stand shall be of hammered work. Its shaft, its branches, its bowls, its ornamen-

tal knobs, and flowers shall be of one piece. And six branches shall come out of its sides: three branches of the lamp stand out of one side, and three branches of the lamp stand out of the other side. Three bowls shall be made like almond blossoms on one branch, with an ornamental knob and a flower, and three bowls made like almond blossoms on the other branch, with an ornamental knob and a flower – and so for the six branches that come out of the lamp stand. On the lamp stand itself, four bowls shall be made like almond blossoms, each with its ornamental knob and flower. And there shall be a knob under the first two branches of the same, a knob under the second two branches of the same, and a knob under the third two branches of the same, according to the six branches that extend from the lamp stand. Their knobs and their branches shall be of one piece; all of it shall be one hammered piece of pure gold. You shall make seven lamps for it, and they shall arrange its lamps so that they give light in front of it. And its wick-trimmers and their trays shall be of pure gold. It shall be made of a talent of pure gold, with all these utensils.

Nothing even remotely similar had ever been built. There were no other pattern sources or resources for the lamp stand. Moses had to trust the pattern God gave him. The Lord wants to give new things to the Church now, too, so we don't look like the other entities of the world. Patterns that come straight down from Heaven are unique, astonishing, and new. When we build from heavenly blueprints, we confound the principalities of the earth and release the manifold wisdom of God.

MANIFESTING FRUIT AND GIFTS

The lamp stand had seven pipes similar to the ones Zerubbabel saw that symbolized the seven Spirits of God. However, this lamp stand also had nine different ornaments on the pipes: the three flowers, the three knobs, and the three almond blossom-shaped bowls. Each one of those nine items represent the nine fruits described in Galatians 5:22-23, and the nine gifts of the Holy Spirit examined in 1 Corinthians 12:8-10.

When we flow in the seven Spirits of God, the world will see the fruits and gifts of the Spirit flow through us as never before. The world will see a mighty demonstration of God's power, wisdom, and might. If the world ever needed to see the fruit of the Holy Spirit, it's now.

CHRIST'S DIVINE NATURE

"You shall also make a lamp stand of pure gold. The lamp stand shall be of hammered work." Do you think they took each pipe, cut them out, and then welded them together? No! The Lord was specific that it was not to be molded. They had to hammer it into a lamp stand from one solid piece of gold. The craftsperson would need divine wisdom to create this beautiful piece.

Simon Peter tells us in 2 Peter 1:3-9, that we may be partakers of His divine nature by His divine power, but we're also going to go through challenges that require patience and long-suffering. The tempering work of the Holy Spirit brings forth a divine union of the stature of Christ in us, so that we will begin to flow with the sevenfold Spirit of God through our lives. It took a lot of hammering to mold the candlestick. As lights on the hill (see Matt. 5:14), the candlestick (or lamp stand), we're going to have to go through some transformation, too. However, God promises us the fullness of the Holy Spirit, and when we flow in the sevenfold flow, there will be no limitations.

The center shaft of the lamp stand is Jesus. He is the Mediator (see 1 Tim. 2:5), the One from whom flows oil to give light. The branches are connected. This signifies the divine union with Christ that brings the flow of oil to the six branches.

As Christians, we have received the Holy Spirit of God whose mission it is to bring forth the nature of Him who has come to dwell in us. He enables us to become partakers of the sevenfold Spirit of God. Just as in the lamp stand we see six branches and then one center pipe, the number six represents the number of man. One represents Jesus. There are a total of seven then, which means perfection, fullness, or completeness.

This also represents the union of Christ. *It is no longer I who lives but He who lives in me.* We become one with Him. Apart from Him, we can do nothing (see John 15:5). All of the pipes—wisdom and understanding, counsel and might, and knowledge and the fear of the Lord—are dependent on the center pipe, Jesus. We must stay plugged into the center pipe, the presence of Jesus, because communion with Him will release fresh oil and fresh anointing and keep the seven flames burning in our lives.

All of this was a shadow of what is to come. Through the divine union by the Holy Spirit, we become partakers of His divine nature. We know that He received the Spirit of the Lord without measure. Jesus received the fullness of the seven Spirits of God (see Rev. 3:1). He is the Head (see Eph. 1:22-23), and the unlimited anointing was poured out upon Him. That same unlimited anointing is for us today.

WE ARE BURNING LAMPS

It's clear from Revelation 4:5, that the burning lamp stand and His seven Spirits are one and the same: *"And from the throne came flashes of lightning and the rumble of thunder. And in front of the throne were seven lamp-stands with burning flames. They are the seven Spirits of God"* (NLT).

All of the lamp stands we've covered so far are the same; they're God's lamp stands. We are the lamp stand, and when we plug into the fullness of the seven Spirits of God, *we* are that *glorious burning lamp that stands before the throne in the presence of the Father.*

SEATED IN HEAVENLY PLACES

Every spiritual blessing has been given to us in the heavenly places (see

Eph. 1:3). We are not going to grovel in the earthly realm but we are going to be seated in the heavenly places with the Lord. Every believer will be ministering out of the Throne Room. Jesus ministered out of that realm. We will, too.

What flows out of the Throne Room? Rivers flow. What was before the throne? These seven functions or operations of the Holy Spirit always come in pairs after the Spirit of the Lord upon us. I believe the pairing ties in somehow to the pairing of the olive trees Zerubbabel saw in his vision. Counsel pairs with might, wisdom with understanding, and knowledge of the Lord with the fear of the Lord. It's awesome! It's by these pairings, His divine power, and the fullness of the Holy Spirit that we will be partakers of His divine nature.

We're entering a time when we won't want anything but the heart and mind of the Father. We are going through a transformation and we have to embrace it, as Paul stresses in Colossians 1:28-29: *"Him we preach, warning every man and teaching every man in all wisdom, that we may present every man perfect in Christ Jesus. To this end I also labor, striving according to His working which works in me mightily."*

Are you hungry for transformation? I know I am. I want to know, hear, see, and be like Jesus. Embrace His work in you so that He can work through you mightily. Embrace the ministry of the Holy Spirit and allow the seven-fold flow to manifest in your life.

As we become one in this divine union, we become obedient to His voice, and every time we submit our will to His, there's a union. We engage spirit to Spirit, and this engages the King and enthrones Him in the kingdom of our hearts. When we plug into the center pipe, we receive the fresh oil of Psalms 92:10, and as the fresh oil pours in from the Word, the anointing pours into the vat and we become partakers of that rich flow of the unlimited anointing of the Holy Spirit.

Fresh oil feeds the flames—the seven flames atop the seven pipes. It has to be a continuous flow of oil for the seven flames to burn. We trim the wick and replenish the oil in perpetual communion with Him, and the flame burns in divine union with Him. As we advance in the flow of the seven-fold Spirits of God, the fullness of the Holy Spirit, the flow increases. The greater the flow of oil—the greater the flame. The greater the flame—the greater the favor and influence.

SEVEN SPIRITS OF GOD OVERVIEW

The Holy Spirit wants to bring forth the mature stature of Christ in us through the sevenfold functions of His Spirit flowing through us. The seven Spirits of God bestow on us a perpetual flow of His manifest presence, wisdom and understanding, counsel and might, knowledge and fear of the Lord.

The first of the sevenfold operation of the Holy Spirit is the Spirit of the Lord upon (see Isa. 11:2). This speaks of the Lord resting upon us and covering us with His Holy presence. It is our being clothed with Christ (see Gal. 3:27). In Mark 9:2-7, we read about the Lord's transfiguration accompanied by God's holy presence. We are to be clothed with His presence. In Acts 10:38, we see how God anointed Jesus with the Holy Spirit and with power, but with the Holy Spirit upon Him.

The second Spirit, of wisdom, is creative ability to do the impossible; it puts the "wow" factor into our works. It's ability beyond our own ability. It's God's thoughts and ideas in action.

The Spirit of understanding partners with wisdom to help us understand how to mobilize and implement heavenly blueprints and patterns. It's putting two-and-two together and making it happen. The Spirit of understanding also helps us articulate the revelation of His Word that we've been shown. Without understanding, we won't know what to do with those heavenly blueprints.

Paul tells us in Ephesians 1:17-19 what wisdom and understanding partnered do: *"That the God of our Lord Jesus Christ, the Father of glory, may give to you the spirit of wisdom and revelation in the knowledge of Him, the eyes of your understanding being enlightened; that you may know what is the hope of His calling, what are the riches of the glory of His inheritance in the saints, and what is the exceeding greatness of His power toward us who believe, according to the working of His mighty power."*

The Spirit of Counsel is engaging the One who is the Alpha and the Omega. It's listening for and heeding His counsel. The counsel of the Lord stands forever. As we build by His heavenly plans, God releases fresh flows of His counsel, His thoughts, and the intents of His heart.

Counsel then releases the might of God to impart vigor, power, strength, and the anointing to see His divine plans through. With the might of God, we won't just look for the finger of God or His hand, we'll look for His arm—unlimited power and strength! God's might and power are always associated with counsel. The prophet Isaiah called Him Wonderful, Counselor, and Mighty God. We never flow in God's might or power without His wonderful counsel.

The Spirit of knowledge of the Lord is that place of divine union when we come into that place of the deep thoughts of God. It's the place of knowing Him. It's not just His counsel, wisdom or understanding—it's knowing Him—it's the intimate knowledge of Him. Knowledge of Him releases understanding, wisdom, counsel, and might. As we grow in His knowledge, peace and grace multiply, as does our humility. As we increase in our knowledge of His vastness, His depth, His greatness, His awesomeness, His majestic splendor, we sever limitations and the impossible becomes possible, the ordinary extraordinary. In the knowledge of these things, we embrace His counsel with joy. Because we know Him we celebrate wisdom, because we know that He can do all things.

As the Spirit of knowledge flows, it releases a deep and reverent fear of the

Lord. Nothing will foster this godly fear like knowledge of His awesome attributes and His sovereign majesty. Knowledge of who He really is brings a holy fear that takes you to a completely new spiritual level.

Without the sevenfold Spirits of God operating in our lives, we in essence, disable ourselves because we succumb to our natural limitations. God offers us supernatural ability and power to fulfill our destinies and His plans for us with unlimited resources. God will partner with us, as He did with Zerubbabel and Moses, to confound the world. God gave Zerubbabel and Moses the full measure of the Holy Spirit and they flowed in a constant river of wisdom and understanding, counsel and might, knowledge and reverent fear of the Lord.

God spoke great words of encouragement to Zerubbabel through the vision He gave Zechariah, and He speaks those same words even now to the building of His living temple: *"The hands of Zerubbabel have laid the foundation of this temple; His hands shall also finish it. Then you will know that the LORD of hosts has sent Me to you. For who has despised the day of small things"* (Zech. 4:9-10)?

GOD IS LOVE AND LIGHT

It is important to understand that God is both Love and Light. It is not that He gives life and gives love. He *is* Love and He *is* Life.

> *And we know (understand, recognize, are conscious of, by observation and by experience) and believe (adhere to and put faith in and rely on) the love God cherishes for us. God is love, and he who dwells and continues in love dwells and continues in God, and God dwells and continues in him* (1 John 4:16).

> *This is the message we have heard from Him and announce to you, that God is Light, and in Him there is no darkness at all* (1 John 1:5).

Love and light are powers. They are energies that flow as a life-giving river of pure love, and that love becomes incredible light-possessing power to heal, restore and transform. It becomes a river of the love of God, and when we drink of it, we become beings of light—sons and daughters dispersing and flowing in the Light of Love. Until we are flowing in this river and it flows from us—we will not have access to the Tree of Life for the healing of nations.

> …*Jesus stood, and He cried in a loud voice, If any man is thirsty, let him come to Me and drink! He who believes in Me (who cleaves to and trusts in and relies on Me) as the Scripture has said, from his innermost being shall flow [continuously]* **springs** *and* **rivers** *of living water"* (John 7:37- 38).

We need to ask ourselves some questions! What is flowing out of me? What *kind* of light or what kind of sound is flowing out of me? Is it the sound of a bright brilliant light or a dim dark light? The spirit realm of demons and angels see it and know exactly what we are by the brilliance or dimness of that light. Wherever we go, we leave behind a trail of light. We affect people by what we emanate. If we emanate love's light, it will be so bright that it will transform our lives and the people we touch. Why? Because love is an essence, a power, and life. I stated this in my last book, *Glory Rising*, when a person dies, he or she leaves behind a trail of what has emanated from his or her life both negative and positive. Yes, we will leave behind a deposit in this world of the things, people, and circumstances we have touched. Nobody lives or dies unto himself (see Rom. 14:7). We have an effect on this life, on creation, on our world, in which we live.

THE KINGDOM THAT IS IN LIGHT

The Kingdom of God is a Kingdom of pure light. Angles ascend and descend from this realm bringing miracles, healings, impartations and anointings necessary for the moment we are in. It's important for us to understand that the Kingdom of God is a Kingdom that consists of supernatural light. This light created everything that we see in the natural. The Scriptures teach us that God is Light.

> *This is the message we have heard from Him and announce to you, that God is Light, and in Him there is no darkness at all* (1 John 1:5).

And that we are "Sons of Light."

> *For you are all sons of light and sons of the day; we do not belong either to the night or to darkness* (1 Thess. 5:5).

As sons of Light we share an inheritance that is in the Light. Colossians 1:12 says,

> *Giving thanks to the Father, Who has qualified and made us fit to share the portion which is the inheritance of the saints (God's holy people) in the Light.*

So, God is Light, we are sons of Light, and we share an inheritance with God that is in the Kingdom of light. It's all about being invigorated by the light, being strengthened by the light. What is this light? It is the light of the Glory of God. As we look into the light of the Glory of God we are strengthened and invigorated. Verse 12 affirms us in this: "*Giving thanks to the Father who has qualified and made us fit to share the portion which is the inheritance of the saints in the light.*" Your inheritance and your portion, your place where you're strengthened and invigorated in the Holy Spirit of God comes from the Kingdom of light. Because we, along with God, are light.

JESUS THE LIFE AND LIGHT OF MEN

Jesus is both Light and Love. Let's look at John 1:1-4:

In the beginning before all things was the Word, which was Christ. And, the Word was with God and the Word was God. All things were made and came into existence through Him, the Word. And, without Him there was not one thing made that has come into being. In Him was life and the life was the light of men. In Him was life, the Word, and that life was the light of men.

He is light. God is light. Verse 5 goes on to day, "*And, the light shines on the darkness for the darkness has never overpowered it....*" Devils can't stand the light of the Glory of God. Sickness and disease in this physical realm can't handle the supernatural light of heaven. When light from heaven comes into the natural realm, everything in the room changes. Every inferior realm, every dark vibration, every dark demon of hell is exposed and dismissed by the power of the light of the Glory of God. In Him was life and that life was light. When we are born again, literally, we are filled with the Kingdom of light. When you become born again, your spirit man, which was dark and dead, instantaneously becomes filled with the light of heaven and the Glory of God is downloaded into your spirit man. You become a new creature in Christ with a brand new spirit nature. Colossians 1:13 says,

The Father has delivered and drawn us to Himself, out of the control and the dominion of darkness and He has transferred us into the kingdom of the son of His love.

We have been snatched out of the kingdom of darkness and have been transferred, translated or transported into the Kingdom of light and have become light in the world. So this light of the Glory of God illuminates us and gives us access to share the portion with Him, which is our inheritance in the light. The problem is getting past the spirit of the mind that needs to be renewed. The Apostle Paul wrote:

But whenever a person turns [in repentance] to the Lord, the veil is stripped off and taken away. Now the Lord is the Spirit, and where the Spirit of the Lord is, there is liberty (emancipation from bondage, freedom). And all of us, as with unveiled face, [because we] continued to behold [in the Word of God] as in a mirror the glory of the Lord, are constantly being transfigured into His very own image in ever increasing splendor and from one degree of glory to another; [for this comes] from the Lord [Who is] the Spirit (2 Cor. 3:16-18).

"Where the spirit of the Lord is there is liberty," refers to freedom from the shackles of the mind. And, we all with unveiled faces, as we continue to engage the Glory where our inheritance is, and as we continue to stare into the light of the Glory of God, we are being lifted above into the light of the Glory of His presence. In that place, He transforms your memories. He transforms the DNA, the spiritual fabric, the way that you understand who God is, and who you are, and the one who lives in you. You start to believe. Satan does not want you to get this revelation. All of the unseen realm of the light of the Glory of God lives inside of you as a supernatural creature.

SOUND IS THE ORIGIN OF LIGHT

Sound is the origin of light. For years now, science has always understood that an atom broken down to its most finite state is nothing more than concentrated light form. But even more recently they have discovered that light can be broken down further. Light reduced to its most infant form is what science calls *vibrating super cells of sound*. So then, sound is the basis of all life. Scripture confirms this in Genesis 1:1-3:

IN THE beginning God (prepared, formed, fashioned, and) created the heavens and the earth. The earth was without form and an empty waste, and darkness was upon the face of the very great deep. The Spirit of God was moving (hovering, brooding) over the face of the waters. And God said, Let there be light; and there was light.

God's voice is the base formula along with the matter of earth and the creative matter or power of the brooding Holy Spirit. When God *spoke*, the vibration from the sound of His voice brought forth light. So if light comes from sound, then sound must be the origin of color. This is how we can understand, prophetically speaking, that color has a sound. Sound has a color, and color has a sound. Stay with me now!

The motion picture industry reveals much about the color of sound. Drama, romance, and horror movie scores all project sound that is congruent to what is being projected on the main screen. The music is the emotion, or the spirit force, that carries the impact of what is being viewed. The color of the music, whether dark or light, is applied to project theatrics. The power of certain sounds as they have been applied in your earlier life can pull you back into the emotion of a place you thought you had left years ago. Do you remember the movie Jaws? Two notes have brought fear into the lives of countless swimmers to this day. Recently I was water skiing and took a spill on a Lake in northern Wisconsin. As I came to the surface and looked around at the vast size and depth of that lake, all I could here were those two haunting piano notes… dune dune… dune dune…. For a moment I was petrified.

The power of sound produces emotion. Just as there are dark sounds, there are light sounds. There are devilish dark sounds and colors, and there are heavenly light sounds and color. We need to be creating an environment by praise and thanksgiving that will pull heaven to earth and flood our churches, cities and regions with the Light of the Glory of God. When this happens true revival will take place. We won't have to advertise revival—revival will be in the air!

ATTRACTING & REPELLING THE LIGHT OF THE GLORY REALM

When we manifest faith we are emitting a power and a brilliance that will attract heaven. However, when we manifest unbelief, in the form of depression or discouragement, the light of the Glory realm fades. Praise is a glorious golden light that manifests in the realm of the spirit. Often we see gold dust and golden oil come in this type of environment. Thanksgiving is this kind of power and Glory. When we are thankful it opens up the gates of heaven for everything of which we have need. When we moan and grumble about things in our lives it attracts a demonic power that will cut us off from heaven and eventually, will even affect the cells in our body and the marrow in our bones.

A joyful heart is good medicine (Prov. 17:22).

Sickness is a vibration that works against the body and causes it to decompose. Faith and thanksgiving are a powerful vibration that destroys sickness when exercised. When we choose to be thankful, a heavenly glorious light and power will fill us and transform us right down to the cells in our body. If we are always talking about sickness, we'll be surrounded by the vibration and demonic power of that sickness. We need to stop talking about sickness! You may feel sick but stop energizing the sickness by talking about it. Thank God for all the good things in your life and forget sickness and it will die. Depression and self-pity attracts a dark presence that will cut you off from the light of the Glory of God and destroy you. Give thanks to God in everything and in every situation and watch your circumstances instantly change. Watch your body gain new strength and power.

...giving thanks to the Father, who has qualified us to share in the inheritance of the saints in Light (Col. 1:12, NASB).

...God is Light, and in Him there is no darkness at all (1 John. 1:5).

He [God] wraps himself in light as with a garment... (Psalm 104:2, NIV, emphasis mine).

[The Father] has delivered and drawn us to Himself out of the control and the dominion of darkness and has transferred us into the kingdom of the Son of His love [the Kingdom of Light]... (Col. 1:13; emphasis mine).

ATTITUDES ARE A LIGHT ENERGIZING POWER

Attitudes also have the power to either attract or repel the presence and power of God. When we begin to praise God, we immediately become surrounded with heavenly light and Glory. The spirit world knows who we are—not just by our words, but by the color of light that emanates from us. The New Age community calls it "Aura," but the light they see on us is the light of the Glory of God. Demons and angels need only take one good look at us and know immediately who we are by the light coming from us. These attitudes are a power that pour from us and open up gates that will take us deeper into the emotion and the spirit of an attitude good or bad. It is clearly then our responsibility in everything to overcome with a right attitude and a thankful heart.

> ...*always giving thanks for all things in the name of our Lord Jesus Christ...* (Eph. 5:20).

The Lord said to Job, "...*adorn yourself with glory and splendor, and clothe yourself in honor and majesty*" (Job 40:10, NIV). In the midst of his trials, God told Job to wrap himself in Glory and light and to cloak himself with honor and majesty! What we manifest in attitude and atmosphere will reproduce around us. Happiness is a choice. We choose to produce joy or depression. Which cloak will you wear today?

THOUGHTS BECOME A LIVING LIGHT FORCE

It's important for us to keep in mind that thoughts are seeds that produce light and life. Thoughts have life in them and will reproduce. As we talked about earlier, the *Creation Law of Reproduction* simply means all things reproduce after their own kind. Genesis 1:11-12 says the earth brought forth grass and herbs yielding seed after their kind, and the tree yielding fruit, and the fruit produced seed after its own kind.

Our thoughts aren't momentary insignificant blurbs, but they possess life and power that chart the course of our present and future life. If our thoughts indeed possess this light power then how are these seeds planted?

When a thought firmly connects with emotion, a supernatural power or light force is conceived. If you hold those thoughts until they are mixed with your emotions, desire releases the power of life and light and they birth. This principle is similar to, *"If two of you agree on earth about anything... it shall be done for them"* (Matt. 18:19).

When your emotions agree with your thinking, it shall be done! This is the power of union and agreement. It works for both God-thoughts and demonic thoughts. So be careful what you desire!

Take, for example, love. Your husband or wife comes home from work and gives you a big kiss and tells you with warm affection you are loved. When the connection takes place between your thoughts and your emotions, it begins to fill your entire being and becomes a living force. This seed of thought, when energized by emotion, will literally create an environment of love and joy around your entire household.

Any thoughts that connect with our emotions become a very strong light energizing power and determine the atmosphere around us. The church has taught for years that emotions are not important. However, I say to you that emotions as well as your thought life are the light inspiring creative side of you. Your emotions are essential for everything to happen. Jesus was moved with an emotion called compassion and released miracles (see Matt. 20:34; Mark 1:41). Compassion releases miracles—even the raising of the dead (Luke 7:11-17).

The power and Glory of God in the anointing are released through the gateway of human affection. When our thinking connects with our feelings, a seed is planted by desire and a light power is released.

So we need to be careful what we think.

BE CAREFUL WHAT YOU THINK

We need to be careful what we are thinking! Every time we think, we place a spiritual offering at the door of that thought that energizes and empowers it. Conception takes place when thought and emotion come together. This forms a creative power or bond of agreement that *brings forth* life or death. *Brings forth* means to breed or create, and is the same as a plant that is produced from the seed. It is the Creation Law of Reproduction at work.

When I meditate on the Word and revelation begins to flow, my whole being seems to be flooded with light—not only light, but flooded with the tranquil peace and life of God. The revelation that is coming from God's mind flows through my emotions and is making a place in my spirit man for seed to be planted and grow.

Revelation isn't just an abstract thought; it is a living Light force connected with a feeling buried deep inside of us. When these seeds are planted conception has taken place, and if watered, the revelation will grow and eventually give birth in our life. As a man thinks… so he will become!

BE CAREFUL WHAT YOU SPEAK

Scripture says in Proverbs 18:21 that,

> *Death and life are in the power of the tongue, and they who indulge in it shall eat the fruit of it for life or death.*

When your mind and words lose the power to curse, you will gain access to the Tree of Life. Only those who overcome the darkness will eat of the Tree.

A gentle tongue (with its healing power) is a tree of life, but willful contrariness in it breaks down the spirit (Prov. 15.4).

The King James Version of this verse translates as, "*A wholesome tongue is a tree of life: but perverseness therein is a breach in the spirit.*"

One definition for the word *breach* is "a break in relations." In the above verse it means to be *cut off from abiding in Him*. A wholesome tongue transmits a tree of life but perverseness will cause a breach in the spirit—and this breach cuts you off from God and the light of His love flowing through you. The mouth is the clearest revelation of someone's heart.

The good man out of the good treasure of his heart brings forth what is good; and the evil man out of the evil treasure brings forth what is evil; for his mouth speaks from that which fills his heart (Luke 6:45).

Chapter 7

REVELATION, MATTER, FAITH & FREQUENCY

Just as there are two forms of light, natural and supernatural, so there are two different forms of sounds, the sound in heaven and the sound on the earth. The sound of earth is cluttered with human and demonic debris that can only be changed by the Holy Spirit. These dark earthly sounds can carry a frequency or vibration that works against our spirit, soul and body to break it down and imprison it. Satan is known as the *prince of the power of the air* in Ephesians 2, and his attempt is to keep us from harmony with the voice of the Spirit of God. But we must rise above the noise of the world and ascend into the new sounds of heaven. Isaiah 60:1-3 says:

> ARISE [from the depression and prostration in which circumstances have kept you--rise to a new life]! Shine (be radiant with the glory of the Lord), for your light has come, and the glory of the Lord has risen upon you! For behold, darkness shall cover the earth, and dense darkness [all] peoples, but the Lord shall arise upon you [O Jerusalem], and His glory shall be seen on you. And nations shall come to your light, and kings to the brightness of your rising.

Isaiah said we can rise from the depression or the noise of the earth and come into the Glory. Darkness covers the earth and the people, but—His Glory shall be seen on you—when we *rise* and *shine*. Then the nations will come to the light they see on us, even kings will come to the brightness of *our rising…* but we must rise above… we must ascend and live from above.

LEVELS OF ASCENSION

In our meetings we need to remember one thing, the level of ascension that we enter into in praise will determine the level of miracles we will see manifest in the room. If the ascent isn't high enough, it will make the difference between migraines being healed, or body parts being recreated. There are times in our personal lives and meetings that there's been no atmosphere, sense of the Presence of God, or ascension into His Presence, but we're looking for the Glory of God. The secret to ascending higher in the Glory of God is praise! You PRAISE, PRAISE, PRAISE… until you and your region are changed.

How long should it take for you to walk into a meeting and be in the presence of God? IMMEDIATELY. Is it the amount of songs you sing? No its not. Some of the songs we sing grieve the Spirit. High Praise is what brings you before the face of God. I don't want to just come occasionally before the face of God, but I want to learn to live in the very Presence of God.

THE RELEASE OF ANOINTED FREQUENCIES

New sounds are constantly being released from heaven on the Earth, and along with them an increase of angelic activity. There are dark sounds being released as well. That's why you've got to watch what your children are listening too, because with each dark sound that is released on the Earth there is a demonic power released through it. Listen to me, if dark frequencies can release demon power, then what does the new song release in the church? The new song releases anointed frequencies and angelic activity. The reason angels have not come forth in might and in power is because they're not hearing the anointed sound in the church. When that sound is there, you're going to see angelic activity like you've never seen before. Angels respond according to what they hear coming out of our mouths. What sound is on your voice?

When you're anointed, you have something on your voice that nobody else has unless they are anointed. This is documented. The human voice is made up of atoms; there are atoms in your voice. If atoms are on your voice, then there's matter on your voice. If that is in the natural, what is it like when you get anointed? How much more are the atoms? How much more matter do you have on your voice now that you are anointed? Brother, now that you are anointed, there's enough matter on your voice to speak to the elements of nature.

VOICE PRINT & HIGHER FREQUENCY

Let take this a little bit further. Do you know that when God made man, He tuned man's body to His voice frequency. Every living thing is spinning with the vibration that comes from the voice of the Lord. So your body is spinning and has its form and is even now being sustained by the Voice of His Power. Hebrews 1:13 says that, *"He upholds and maintains all things by the Mighty Word of His Power."*

Sounds either release the demonic or the heavenly. Do you understand why Jesus could walk through a wall? He carried a higher frequency than the wall. Do you know why you can cast out devils? You have a higher frequency. If you don't have a higher frequency, you can't cast it out. Today science calls this *voice print*. Could voice print be the reason why demon powers look at the church and argue with it? Could it be because they know your voiceprint isn't real? Jesus I know Your voice print, but who are they? We want to cast the devil out of someone or something but cannot because the same demonic voiceprint resides in us. The demon says, *"Your voiceprint corresponds with what's in me! You can't cast me out!"*

We must be set free from the very thing we are trying to free others from or we will be powerless to get it done. In other words, how can you cast out that spirit of addiction out of another individual if you have the same thing living in you? If you can't submit to your pastor with that rebellious spirit, how can you expect your children to submit to you?

Do you remember Ella Fitzgerald, who could sing so high she could crack glass? If her natural ability could break matter, what do you really think that praise does in the spirit? Your praise is supposed to break off principalities, it's supposed to break of powers, it's supposed to break up rulers of darkness! Your praise, your voiceprint, your praise level is a natural pulse that can break "glass." And they were not anointed with the miracle working power of God. Do you have any idea what you receive when you received the Holy Ghost? Oh I'm telling you, this thing is dangerous. Demon power knows your voice print. Angels know your voice print. And if you don't have the word of the Lord in your mouth, they won't respond to your words.

Sound also transmits visions, images, and color. When we talk, we often are seeing what people are saying. "I see what you are saying." We don't even realize what we are saying. This means, if the people can't see what you are saying, they haven't heard it. "Faith comes by seeing, and seeing by the word of God." Faith comes by sound. It's important to see what is being spoken.[22]

UNDERSTANDING GOD'S SOUND

You can learn what your gift for healing is when you start filling your life with worship frequencies. People ask me, "Jeff, why do miracles happen so easily in your meetings?" My response is, "Because of the revelation and release of God Sound that brings the atmosphere for miracles to manifest." The Apostle Paul wrote:

Yet when we are among the full-grown (spiritually mature Christians who are ripe in understanding), we do impart a [higher] wisdom (the knowledge of the divine plan previously hidden); but it is indeed not a wisdom of this present age or of this world nor of the leaders and rulers of this age, who are being brought to nothing and are doomed to pass away. But rather what we are setting forth is a wisdom of God once hidden [from the human understanding] and now revealed to us by God--[that wisdom] which God devised and decreed before the ages for our glorification [to lift us into the glory of His presence]. None of the rulers of this age or world perceived and recognized and understood this, for if they had, they would never have crucified the Lord of glory (1 Cor. 2:6).

REVELATION BRINGS MANIFESTATION

Manifestations of the Spirit are coded. A person cannot walk in miracles, signs and wonders without revelation. Revelation brings the manifestation. The manifestation confirms that the revelation comes from God. People cannot argue with the miracles. They may be able to argue with your doctrine but they cannot fight miracles!

As Jesus was teaching the power of the Lord was present with Him to heal.

One of those days as He was teaching, there were Pharisees and teachers of the Law sitting by, who had come from every village and town of Galilee and Judea and from Jerusalem. And the power of the Lord was present with Him to heal them (Luke 5:17).

When revelation comes from heaven, there is power for the manifestation. The devil hates revelation because it brings power with it for manifestation and healing. Hosea 6 says that God's people are destroyed for *"lack of knowledge."* Without revelation knowledge there is no empowerment.

WORLDLY INTELLECTUALISM

Intellectualism has become the means by which this present age determines reality. Worldly reasoning has become the meter by which mankind decides what is valid and real and is humanistic at best. This kind of thinking is dangerous and antagonistic toward God. Worldly intellectualism is completely void of faith. Paul said in 1 Corinthians 2:4-5 that his preaching was done by *the power of signs and wonders so that our faith might not rest in men but in the power of God.*

God wants to teach the body of Christ how to access revelation knowledge from the heavens and manifest on earth in substance. When Adam was created he had the mind of God, but when he fell, he traded the mind of God for an earthly mind based on human intellect and reason.

In the Garden of Eden, Adam didn't need faith because he had everything he needed. Faith is required when you are in need. We need faith when things are closed off and need to get them open again. The very first thing God gave Adam was faith — so he could see the place from which he fell. It was the mercy of God for Adam to receive faith from God; otherwise, he would have died from eternal grief. He needed to know that he would once again have access to the realm of Glory from which he was created and from which he fell.

Time and matter became the basis of Adam's reality. This is why our intellect has a problem with anything that cannot be explained by our five senses. But the problem is that not all matter can be seen! And your intellect was never designed to distinguish between the visible and invisible realm. Paul said we look to the things that we cannot see. The unseen realm designed and created the realm that we can detect with our five senses.

It is absolutely mandatory that we must be transformed or renewed in our thinking in order to see the Kingdom of God. Jesus told Nicodemus, *"You must be born again or born from above in order to see the Kingdom of God"*

(John 3:3). We cannot see the Kingdom without first being born from above. We must undergo a complete spiritual metamorphosis of the Spirit in order to see in the Spirit. To undergo a transformation means to be formed back into the original state in which a thing was created. To be renewed is to bring something back to the original state or form when it was new!

Paul said in Ephesians 4:23 to be, *"renewed in the spirit of your mind."* Originally we must have known both realms.

The natural mind can never show you a miracle. Common sense can never make a blind man see or a deaf man hear nor reveal the reality of the Glory realm because common sense tells us that the natural realm is the boundary that defines what is real and what is not.

REVELATION UNLOCKS TIME, SPACE AND MATTER

We have seen countless displays of creative miracles coming from heaven by simply calling them into the natural when heaven is open. When the Glory of God is in the room creative miracles are as easy as *"Only Speak the Word and my servant will be healed."* When heaven is open you can see what is available there and pull it into time and space—and it will manifest.

I was in a meeting in Korea a short time back with 6,000 people present. So many creative miracles took place that we couldn't keep track of them all. The meetings were televised so millions were watching all around Asia and the world. More were healed through television than those in the meetings and the reports poured in. Out of all of the wonderful things God did, I remember on the last night of the meeting I called out that body parts were being recreated in the meeting. Along with the hundreds that came up to testify of miracles, there were several women who came up to testify that each had previously been missing a finger. In the Glory their missing fingers completely grew out and God even went as far as to put the right color fingernail polish on the nail to match the others!

When the heavens are open, all that we have need of is available and is as easy as calling it from the unseen realm into the visible by faith. I didn't think how this was going to happen, I just saw it, spoke it and it happened.

REVELATION KNOWLEDGE

I don't think any of us really understands just exactly what Adam experienced when he fell from the Glory of God. When Adam fell he traded the mind of Christ for the mind of reason. He went from experiential eating of the Tree of Life to eating from the tree of self-recognition and common sense. Common sense wants you to think and reason, but faith wants you to simply believe and act. This is why our intellect has problems with anything that cannot be explained. Not all matter is visible to the naked eye. Common sense basis reality on what is detected in the five natural senses, but this type of thinking or observation is incomplete.

God is Spirit! When God starts showing us what He wants to bring from the unseen realm of the Glory we need to start speaking it down and manifesting the miracle in the natural. God is looking for a people who will move in revelation that will manifest heaven on the earth, and He is working with people in this generation and this time to bring it about.

The society that we live in is largely educated to what we detect in our physical surrounding, and if we go beyond it we cannot conceive it. The only thing that can take you past your intellect is revelation knowledge. Jesus said in Mark 4:11,

> To you has been entrusted the mystery of the kingdom of God (that is, the secret counsels of God which are hidden from the ungodly); but for those outside (of our circle) everything becomes a parable.

Revelation knowledge is the only thing that can bring us to the place of seeing the unseen realm. The natural mind and intellect can't do it. They are two completely different frequencies. The natural mind is completely incompatible with the mind of the Spirit. Common sense can't show you how to make a blind man see or a dead man live. Only revelation knowledge can show you these possibilities and realities. We need the mind of Christ! Common sense says the physical realm is the boundary by which we are to define reality and anything beyond that the mind cannot comprehend or believe. But a generation is rising that does not determine reality based upon what it can detect with the five senses, but rather determines reality based upon the Word of God and revelation knowledge.

THE SPIRIT REALM AND RESURRECTION GLORY

Hebrews says that the things that we see with the natural eye were created by the things that we cannot see. They are made of unseen matter. The spirit realm holds matter together and maintains it. This applies to both the demonic realm as well as the supernatural Kingdom of God. Sickness is upheld by demonic tones or vibrations. The father of lies speaks as well! If he can get us to agree with him and with his voice he can bring sickness upon us—but in order for that to happen we must first agree to it. You see, we have the final say-so on the outcome of our lives! By our words we are justified and by our words we are condemned.

As the Glory of God increases in the earth in the days to come there will be an explosion of the raising of the dead. When Jesus was raised from the grave on the third day, Scripture tells us that there was a mighty earthquake that shook the earth so violently that it opened up the graves, and many saints were seen walking through the streets of Jerusalem testifying to the resurrection of the Lord Jesus Christ. There was such a Glory released at the resurrection that those who had died in the Lord rose from their graves and were witnessed preaching in the streets. Now that's resurrection Glory! Death is nothing more than the spirit realm divorcing itself from physical realm. The Spirit realm is the real realm that causes life and breath to exist in the natural. When the spiritual breaks away from the natural there is death. So, when the manifest presence of Almighty God is present in our atmosphere, that which is dead will be resurrected! When the true Spirit of God invades an atmosphere, all that is dead will get up. The raising of the dead will be the most common miracle done by common people in the coming Glory Revival.

BREAKING DEMONIC FREQUENCIES

I was in a meeting last year in New Zealand in which the Spirit of the Lord moved powerfully with many creative miracles manifesting in the room. Testimony after testimony came forth of wonderful miracles of instantaneous healings from the Presence of the Lord. When the meeting was over a man approached me from the back of the auditorium and said that he had brought his wife in the service. They had sat in the back during most of the meeting as she was not able to get up; her pain was so extreme. He proceeded to tell me that she had been suffering from stage four melanoma cancer and that the doctors gave her only two to four weeks to live. He asked me if I would pray for her and I agreed. As the woman approached the front of the building I could smell her before she came into focus. The stench of the spirit of cancer had engulfed her. She looked weak, weighing less than 100 pounds, and wearing a scarf as all of her hair had fallen out from the chemotherapy. Her husband helped put her in the chair in the front row seat and then they turned their attention toward me. As I began to walk toward her I could feel the resistance from the spirit of cancer that was consuming her body; yet, as I looked at her something different happened. I spoke to the woman and said, "Honey, you don't have cancer! The doctors were wrong! You're going to be just fine." Without touching her, I turned around and walked away. I couldn't help but think that my actions appeared quite abrupt or even rude.

Several months later the pastors from that church in Auckland, New Zealand came to our 2010 Power and Glory of the Kingdom event in Murfreesboro, Tennessee. Immediately, Pastor Tim approached me and said,

"Hey Jeff, great to see you! Do you remember the woman that you prayed for at the end of the last event at our church last year?" I had to think for a moment.

"Yes, I remember the lady that came forward with her husband who was eaten up with cancer," I replied.

He said, "That's the one. I just wanted to let you know that all of her hair has grown back in and last week she went back to work at her old job. The doctors said she is a living miracle as all of the cancer in her body miraculously disappeared!"

Proverbs 18:6 says, *"Life and death are in the power of the tongue."*

What happened was that this woman received a bad report from her doctor and then agreed with it, making it a powerful demonic decree. We need to be careful what we are agreeing with. In Mark 5, when Jarius received the report that his little girl was dead, Scripture states that Jesus overheard the report, but ignored it. He spoke to the heart and mind of Jarius and said, *"...keep on believing Jarius."* The power of agreement is key. We need to be agreeing with the Word and the voice of the Spirit, and as we do we will cancel out the voice of the enemy and break demonic agreements meant for our destruction. The doctors may be right in diagnosing a situation and it may be a fact that you have a particular condition. But there is a higher truth available to us than plain fact. It's called "By His Stripes I am healed." Truth in the Word trumps fact every time.

THE COMING SUPER SHIFT

The heavens are a symphony, declaring the will of God for the earth. The universe is a cosmic time piece revealing times and seasons that we need to be familiar with. God has a Cosmic Calendar that reveals times and seasons to the sons of men and there is a Super Shift coming upon this generation that will manifest heaven on earth like no other generation before us. This may sound strange to some, but it was God who placed the starts in the heavens causing them to follow His course of action and reveal His timings to us, not Satan. David writes:

THE HEAVENS declare the glory of God; and the firmament shows and proclaims His handiwork (Ps. 19:1).

Long before Astrologers and the New Age community twisted our perception of the heavens, there has been a witness of the stars and the constellations that confirm the accuracy of biblical prophetic truths. Daniel had understanding of this, as well as Job, regarding the Zodiac, Orion's Belt and the Bear in Job 38. Three wise men (astrologers) came from the east following a "Star" that pointed them to the Christ. Daniel revealed these things centuries before and "wise men" remembered and counted the time that this heavenly King would be born, right down to the very day! I would love to go into further details of these truths but then again, this is another book! I will say this—the heavens are singing and declaring the Glory of God Now!

THE ORIGINAL PATTERN FOR CREATION

According to science, sound and frequency are the exact same thing, but matter and frequency are different components and need each other to work. If you change the frequency in gold, the molecular structure will change and cause it to become a liquid. If you change the frequency of water, it will become a gas. In order to work in the miraculous we need to understand we have authority to change and reclaim the natural through revelation declarations.

In Genesis, God said, "Let there be..." and the universe came from the sound of His voice. God called light from the unseen realm and the frequency of that light was His voice. He spoke, and it began to resonate and it became light. Light, energy, matter, then the universe and here we are—all from His voice. So everything we see in the natural came from God-sound or God-frequency.

If you develop a mole on your arm, that mole is merely a frequency that changed the molecular structure of your tissue from the original frequency. When we think of frequency we automatically think of sound, but frequency goes far beyond what we hear with our ears.

What we set our eyes upon and allow into our mind is what will manifest in and around us. According to the *"Law of Focus,"* seeing produces thought which in turn produces a Light Power that energizes seeds of desire. When these seeds reach maturity they will bring forth according to their design. What you focus on will literally chart the course of your present and future for good or bad. If you hold those thoughts until they are mixed with your emotions, desire releases the power of life and light and they birth. This principle is similar to, *"If two of you agree on earth about anything… it shall be done for them…"* (Matt. 18:19).

This is the power of union and agreement. This applies to God-thoughts, fleshly desires, and demonic thoughts. So be careful little eyes what you see! Jesus said to be careful how you look upon a woman because your future is connected to what you see.

According to scientific study and mentioned in David Van Koovering's audio message, "The Science of God Sound," when you see something, your brain responds with 700 times more fire power than when you heard a sound. This means that the eye gate is 700 times more powerful than the ear gate. So if we limit God to hearing Him by sound alone we are not hearing very much and are missing most of what He is saying.[23]

Sin has a sound frequency as well and can bring you under the power of its voice. It will manifest around you as a dark light, which will pull an individual deeper into its power if not repented of by renouncing and changing the frequency. Now the Glory of God is the original pattern that everything consists of. The universe and the Cosmos have their original set design from the Voice of the Lord but were drastically changed by the fall of Lucifer first, then the fall of man. God's Cosmic Realm, the Glory Realm, is still the original pattern for creation and will ultimately reframe and restore all that has been altered... but that's another book!

GOD KNEW YOU BEFORE TIME

There was never a time that you were not in the mind of God. From the beginning, before your birth, He knew you. Before you had this dirt body, and the atomic structure that forms your shape—God knew you and was singing your song frequency. We are eternal, and birthed by an eternal God given a destiny and a holy calling to be fulfilled from before the foundation of the world.

[For it is He] Who delivered and saved us and called us with a calling in itself holy and leading to holiness not because of anything of merit that we have done, but to further His own purpose and grace (unmerited favor) which was given us in Christ Jesus before the world began [eternal ages ago] (2 Tim. 1:9).

Before the worlds were framed and placed into their cosmic order we existed and were given a holy calling and destiny to be fulfilled for this planet. Not only that, but we were completely known by Him. We are not some invaluable thing abortion can snuff the life frequency out of. God knew our framework before our mother's womb. He has a destiny, a purpose, and a plan for us, though many miss it.

If we have faith we can see what God sees, using spiritual perception to know what He knows. It is in this place that you can see yourself in a different light and that revelation will change your world.

For as he thinks in his heart, so is he (Prov. 23:7).

As you see what God observes, your framework will change—calling the nonexistent things as though they already are. It's all about frequency.

THE HARMONIOUS FREQUENCY OF THE GLORY REALM

How full of the Spirit are you? Do you have capacity enough to see your future? This isn't *New Age*—it's *Kingdom Age*. By the anointing you know all things:

> *But you have been anointed by [you hold a sacred appointment from, you have been given an unction from] the Holy One, and you all know [the Truth] or you know all things* (1 John 2:20).

When the fall took place the molecular structure of creation changed in an instant of time and man lost his ability to know his destiny as a heavenly citizen. But you've got a memory, you can remember yesterday, you have an anointing from the Holy One and by faith you can be lifted up to see the place from which you fell—from the realm of Glory.

For all have sinned and have fallen short of the Glory of God (Rom. 3:23).

Romans clearly states, that when Adam fell in the garden, he fell from a place. That place was called the Glory of God. We can be restored to *the Glory of God* by faith in Jesus Christ. Jesus said that when the Holy Spirit comes, you will know all things; you will know all truth. He'll only speak the things He has heard from the Father, and He will show you things to come—for they are printed on your spirit man, and you will see what God sees, and know your destiny.

The Glory Realm is here! We're not tuned in to it because we are too much in our own mind and not the mind of Christ. We need to let God speak His voice, His science, His frequency, His sound into us and we will be complete. He made you a certain way. Find out what God has spoken over your life to become and resonate there. Don't try to be something you are not. Find out what it is that He designed you to be and you'll flourish.

Chapter 8

THE ROAR OF
THE LORD

Not long ago, I traveled to Australia for a series of meetings beginning in Melbourne and ending in Adelaide. The first night of the last leg of our stay in Adelaide, the Lord told me, "Jeff, tonight I want you to get the people to release the Roar of the Lord over the nation of Australia, for I am about to shift the government of My Kingdom here, which will result in an increase in the miraculous." So, toward the end of the worship I took the microphone and said, "Tonight, the Lion of the Tribe of Judah is going to Roar over the nation of Australia. The Lord said that He was going to shift His Government tonight in the realm of the Spirit and that it will bring an increase of authority, which will literally result in a release of new miracles. So tonight we are going to release the Roar of the Lord!"

I told them that when a lion wants to assert his dominance in a region he does not lift his head and roar into the air, but rather he lowers his head and releases a mighty roar into the ground. When he does that, the vibration of that roar travels for miles around and everything in the jungle is on high alert, for the vibrations or that roar lets everyone know that he is king of the jungle.

I told the people to stand in the midst of worship and as they did, I began to prophecy:

"Tonight the Lord is going to Roar through His people! There is a Lion living in your belly. He is the Lion of the Tribe of Judah and He has won the right to assert His dominion through you and over this nation! Tonight as we Roar in the Spirit there is going to be a shift in the Government of God in Australia that will be felt by the shaking of the ground in Melbourne, Adelaide and Perth. For the ground will shake as a sign in the natural that I am shifting My government and confirming it with signs that are outside the reach of man to confirm. And you will know that it is I that am at work in this nation says the Spirit of the Lord!"

Then, on the count of three, we released the Roar of the Lord. There was such a release of power in the auditorium that people shook all over and laid on the ground. Before the service was over that night, people were receiving text messages that an earthquake had hit in Melbourne. Earthquakes are unlikely in the nation of Australia. Within a few short days all three cites, Melbourne, Adelaide and Perth shook under the power of earthquakes that were reported by the news stations and papers as highly unusual. God was confirming His Word with tangible signs in the natural from the release of the Roar of the Lord.

TRUCKEE, CALIFORNIA

Several years prior to this event I told a friend, Eric Moen, from Truckee, California that the Lord was going to release His roar and shake the mountain region he was in as a sign that revival was coming to his region. The prophetic was something that was new to him so he basically just agreed with me as I was prophesying to him over the phone. Immediately, the mountains began to shake and within the days and weeks that followed close to a thousand small quakes occurred in the region. I called Eric back on the phone and asked him if the mountain was shaking enough for him yet. Needless to say he was amazed at the immediate release of power on the word.

RELEASING THE ROAR OF THE LORD

God is releasing a Roar in His people in this season. The Lion of the Tribe of Judah is literally roaring through a family of sons on the earth to establish His dominion. The earth will shake as the vibration of His Roar is released causing regions to break out into revival. There is an authority given to the church that will shake the nations of the earth and all will know it is the Lord.

> *The Lord roars out of Zion and utters His voice from Jerusalem* (Amos 1:2).

I believe that Zion is inside of us—a holy hill. Jesus said,

> *The Kingdom of God is both in you, and it's around you* (Luke 17:21).

Joel 3:16 states that the Lord will roar out of Zion, "*The Lord will thunder and roar from Zion and utter His voice from Jerusalem, and the heavens and earth shall shake.*" I believe that in the earth today, the Lord is beginning to roar into the nations of the earth through a corporately anointed Body of Christ.

What we've actually been talking about is the release of the prophetic decree. Atmospheres shift and miracles come out of the decree—the spoken word—because this is the voice of authority and the voice of the Holy Spirit of God. When declarations come out of the sons and daughters of God they are released as a mighty roar in the earth that can be felt by angels, demons and creation itself. Creation is waiting for the coming forth of a family of God on the earth that will speak with such authority the elements respond to them. I've rebuked tornados and have had them dissolve, spoken to the wind and commanded it to do certain things that were witnessed by thousands in events around the nations and even documented on film. As Spirit filled sons of God, we have the right to release the roar of the Lord as family on this planet. You can call it what you want, but in reality it's Christ in you speaking, roaring and establishing His dominion through you.

JESUS CHRIST IS THE LION OF THE TRIBE OF JUDAH SEATTLE, WASHINGTON

Another time as I was ministering at Transformation Center in Seattle, Washington, I began to make faith decrees in a powerful atmosphere of praise. As the faith decrees came forth I saw the head of a very large Lion come into the room. As I looked, the Lion had a crown on the top of His head and He was roaring over the people. I noticed that His eyes were like bright green emeralds with light beaming out of them. As the people were worshiping Him, He was roaring over them. It reminded me of Aslan in C. S. Lewis' series, *The Chronicles of Narnia*. When Aslan roared over the people of stone, they transformed back into flesh and bone. There was something similar happening here. As I was watching this happen, I began to prophesy over the people that the Lion of the Tribe of Judah was roaring over them tonight and that this was a season of resurrection Glory. Resurrection power was beginning to be released in Seattle and God was resurrecting their dead situations back to life.

Emeralds Appear in Mouth

That night I ministered with the worship team behind me, as I often do, and the Glory of God began to manifest in powerful dimensions. Along with all of the wonderful miracles of healing, there was a woman present who is part of the leadership of that local body. She fell to the ground shaking under the anointing and out from her mouth came three beautiful emeralds. This brought the fear of the Lord into the meeting… as signs and wonders often do. The Lord was confirming the vision that I had seen in the realm of the Spirit by signs in the natural. The *Three* was for third day resurrection power, and the *Emeralds* were to confirm that it was the Lion of the Tribe of Judah. I came to find out afterward that Seattle is known as the "Emerald City" and that the stone for the tribe of Judah in the ephod that the High Priest wore on his chest was the emerald. We were all in awe as the Lord confirmed His word with incredible signs in the natural.

ISAIAH 51 GOVERNMENT OF GOD

The Isaiah 9:6-7 government of God is being established in the earth like never before:

> For to us a Child is born, to us a Son is given; and **the government shall be upon His shoulder**, and His name shall be called Wonderful Counselor, Mighty God, Everlasting Father [of Eternity], Prince of Peace. **Of the increase of His government and of peace there shall be no end**, upon the throne of David and over his kingdom, to establish it and to uphold it with justice and with righteousness from the [latter] time forth, even forevermore. The zeal of the Lord of hosts will perform this (Isa. 9:6-7).

The government of the Kingdom of God has been growing now in the earth for over 2,000 years from its infancy in seed-form to a now-mature plant that is ready for harvest—and Jesus Christ will reap the reward of His sufferings.

> The earth produces [acting] by itself—first the blade, then the ear, then the full grain in the ear. But when the grain is ripe and permits, immediately he sends forth [the reapers] and puts in the sickle, because the harvest stands ready (Mark 4:28-29).

The Gospel of the Kingdom is at a place of maturation in the Body of Christ and I believe we are at a place where the Lord will permit the reapers (angels and works) to bring in the harvest. And this will be done with incredible supernatural efficiency and release of consistent power from heaven.

Once, I asked Prophet Bob Jones, "Why aren't miracles consistently happening in the Body of Christ?" He said, "Jeff, it's because there isn't a consistent government on the earth being displayed through a corporate body. There is a government, but there is a more superior government coming that will be released in power through unity. There's a government that comes through brotherhood."

> Oh how good and pleasant it is when brothers dwell together in unity (Ps. 133:1).

When we see this unity come into place, I believe we will see a much more consistent display of power, and miracles. Like it was with Jesus we are going to see the days of "...and He healed them all" (Matt. 12:15, NASB). What would that look like if you or I had that kind of miracle healing anointing where everyone you laid hands on was completely healed? I'm telling you, the world would beat a pathway to your door!

> Nations shall come to your light, and kings to the brightness of your rising (Isa. 60:2).

The nations will come to the brightness of our rising. You are cut from the same stone as your Daddy.

This is also affirmed in Isaiah 51:1:

> HEARKEN TO Me, you who follow after rightness and justice, you who seek and inquire of [and require] the Lord [claiming Him by necessity and by right]: **look to the rock from which you were hewn** and to the hole in the quarry from which you were dug...

Look to the Rock from which you were taken from. We have the same genetics.

> Look to Abraham your father and to Sarah who bore you; for I called

him when he was but one, and I blessed him and made him many (Isa. 51:2).

You are your Father's children, and you are blessed by God. It doesn't matter what you do. You are blessed by God. You can short circuit it, and you can default it; you can dis-acknowledge it and have none of the benefits apply to you. But if you look to the Rock, and you put to remembrance the Lord, all these blessings will follow you.

We are in a place of restoration. I believe God wants to make this place like it was originally intended to look. I believe we are in the place where it is going to look exactly like it was when it was created, when God put Adam in the middle of the Garden, as earth's first ambassador and governor. The earth will be filled with the knowledge of the Glory of the Lord. The Bible says that God is going to establish His government in the Millennial Reign here on the earth, and God is going to restore all things through the man-God, Jesus Christ, who came to bring the government of God back to the earth through the veil of His flesh, and the shedding of His blood. He opened up the new and living way, so the Kingdom of God could come in a new governmental way. He's in the process of making this place look like His place.

> *Therefore, brethren, since we have full freedom and confidence to enter into the [Holy of] Holies [by the power and virtue] in the blood of Jesus, By this fresh (new) and living way which He initiated and dedicated and opened for us through the separating curtain (veil of the Holy of Holies), that is, through His flesh* (Heb. 10:19-20).

The Lord will make earth look like heaven:

> *For the Lord will comfort Zion; He will comfort all her waste places. And He will make her wilderness like Eden, and her desert like the garden of the Lord. Joy and gladness will be found in her, thanksgiving and the voice of song or instrument of praise. Lift up your eyes to*

the heavens, and look upon the earth beneath (Isa. 51:3, 6).

It's a position of authority. Ephesians 2:6 says,

> *And He raised us up together with Him and made us sit down to-gether [giving us joint seating with Him] in the heavenly sphere [by virtue of our being] in Christ Jesus (the Messiah, the Anointed One).*

Paul is talking about the spiritual temple of the Lord. Zechariah 6:12-13 elaborates on this:

> *And say to him, "Thus says the Lord of hosts: [You, Joshua] behold (look at, keep in sight, watch) the Man [the Messiah] whose name is the Branch, for He shall grow up in His place and He shall build the [true] temple of the Lord. Yes, [you are building a temple of the Lord, but] it is He Who shall build the [true] temple of the Lord, and He shall bear the honor and glory [as of the only begotten of the Father] and shall sit and rule upon His throne. And He shall be a Priest upon His throne, and the counsel of peace shall be between the two [offices—Priest and King]."*

You are building this temple, but there is one coming called the Branch, and He will build the true temple of the Lord. His office is going to be between King and Priest.

SEATED IN HEAVENLY PLACES

Paul also wrote to the church at Ephesus bringing them into this revelation:

> *And He raised us up together with Him and made us sit down to-gether [giving us joint seating with Him] in the heavenly sphere [by virtue of our being] in Christ Jesus (the Messiah, the Anointed One)* (Eph. 2:6).

It's all about rising-up-in. He has raised you up and He has caused you to sit down in the heavenly realm, giving you joint seating. Look up to the Lord, and then look down on the earth; this is your position. You can't rule anything down here if you're not living in the revelation of being seated up above with Christ Jesus. The elements don't have to listen to you, devils don't have to listen to you, sickness and disease don't have to listen to you, but they will listen to the authoritative word of sons and daughters who know their position, place, and from where they rule. You cannot shift anything down here unless you understand where you are seated. It's called the seat of government. Jesus lived and moved from heaven's government, demonstrating Kingdom power, and He said that those of us who lived from and were abiding in Him would be able to do the exact same works of power He did and even greater works!

> *I assure you, most solemnly I tell you, if anyone steadfastly believes in Me, he will himself be able to do the things that I do; and he will do even greater things than these, because I go to the Father* (John 14:12).

Paul said that Jesus is the "...*firstborn among many brothers* (Rom. 8:29, NIV).

In John 3, Jesus tells Nicodemus that he must be born again, which confuses him. Jesus then went on to say, "*That which is born of flesh is flesh, that which is born of Spirit is Spirit, you must be born again.*" Nicodemus is thinking womb, but Jesus is thinking *Wind*. You must be born from the spirit, not the earth. That which is of the earth is born from the earth, but that which is spiritual is born from above.

> *But to as many as did receive and welcome Him, He gave the authority (power, privilege, right) to become the children of God, that is, to those who believe in (adhere to, trust in, and rely on) His name* (John 1:12).

That means trust in, and completely rely on Him—they owe their birth to God, they are born from above. Nicodemus is thinking that he has to be born again on the earth. Meanwhile, Jesus is telling him that it is not the womb, but it is in the Wind. Jesus is trying to explain natural things to Nicodemus, who can't understand earthly things, let alone spiritual. Jesus told Nicodemus,

> If I have told you of things that happen right here on the earth and yet none of you believes Me, how can you believe (trust Me, adhere to Me, rely on Me) if I tell you of heavenly things? And yet no one has ever gone up to heaven, but there is One Who has come down from heaven—the Son of Man [Himself], Who is (dwells, has His home) in heaven (John 3:12-13).

Jesus was ministering on the earth as an authoritative Son, but at the same time standing in the very presence of God, ruling from His position as a Spirit filled Son—the first born among many brothers, displaying by example what you and I have full privilege, right, and ability to function in as Spirit-filled sons and daughters of God.

THE WAKEE, WAKEE ANGEL

We're in a season of Awakening in the nations of the earth as the Lion of Tribe of Judah is roaring. Something fresh is being poured out from the presence of the Lord. At the beginning of the year the Lord told me that we were in a season of the two elevens, or the 11:11. I asked the Lord what this meant, and He referred me to John 11:11:

> He said these things, and then added, Our friend Lazarus is at rest and sleeping; but I am going there that I may awaken him out of his sleep.

The Lord said that in this season He was beginning to wake up Lazarus, which is the sleeping church. The Lord said that the church was dead but He was coming to "Wake her up." Four months prior to the time the Holy Spirit was poured out in the great Welsh revival in 1904-1905, Evan Roberts was pressing into the Presence of the Lord, having nightly visitations. These encounters were accompanied by angelic visitations. The name of the angel that visited Evan was called "Wakee, Wakee." An angel called "Wake Up" was involved in one of the most significant revivals to ever touch that nation and the nations of the earth at that time. The Azusa Street Revival of Los Angeles in 1906 was directly on the heels of the Welsh Revival.

> *Awake, awake, put on strength and might, O arm of the Lord; awake, as in the ancient days, as in the generations of long ago (Isa. 51:9).*

It's time for the Church of Jesus Christ to Wake up! ...Wake up!

> *The Lord God says, "The redeemed of the lord shall return and come with singing to Zion. Everlasting joy shall be upon their heads, and they shall obtain joy and gladness. And sorrow and sighing will flee away (Isa. 51:11).*

So Wake up! Wake up church, for the redeemed of the Lord shall return and is going to make the wilderness look like Eden.

SUPERNATURAL EDEN WILL BLOOM AGAIN

> *For the Lord will comfort Zion; He will comfort all her waste places.* **And He will make her wilderness like Eden, and her desert like the garden of the Lord.** *Joy and gladness will be found in her, thanksgiving and the voice of song or instrument of praise (Isa. 51:3).*

The world needs to know that we are building into something here and now on the earth that will play out significantly in the Millennial Reign in which supernatural Eden will bloom again. God has a plan for us now that will transfer over into the coming Kingdom age and that we are literally building into it now. The decisions we make now carry weight and power for that time. We need to understand that we are called to build a new world. We are not just called to be saved here and now but we are building for a better millennial world.

Most people are just waiting for the time we can get to heaven and get this whole "world thing" over with. How tragic... how boring! We need to have something to aim at and head for. What about the earth? Adam's first assignment as the ruler or as king in the earth was to bring heaven into this place. So we had a mishap! It's only been a 6,000 year side step in the scope of all of eternity. What about the Kingdom mandate to transform the earth? Whatever happened to that? God had never changed His mind or altered the program! Jesus Christ came and brought back the government of that Kingdom and it has been growing in the earth as a mustard seed, first the seed, then the blade and the stalk, until it grows like Jesus said and becomes the largest of all of the plants in the earth so that the birds come and lodge in its branches. The Kingdom of God has been growing and increasing like that for some 2,000 years now, but it will soon come into its full measure in this timeframe called the Millennial Reign of Christ on the earth. The Apostle John saw a new heaven and a new earth:

> THEN I saw a new sky (heaven) and a new earth, for the former sky and the former earth had passed away (vanished), and there no longer existed any sea. And I saw the holy city, the new Jerusalem, descending out of heaven from God, all arrayed like a bride beautified and adorned for her husband (Rev. 21:1-2).

THE SECOND ADAM AND HIS BRIDE

John saw a new heaven and a new earth being created. In the Millennial Reign we will rule with Christ 1,000 years judging the nations and will play a role in the re-creation or transformation of this planet. The original mandate from God to Adam was:

> *God blessed them and said to them, Be fruitful, multiply, and fill the earth, and subdue it [using all its vast resources in the service of God and man]; and have dominion* (Gen. 1:28).

Adam was commissioned by God to fill the earth and "*Subdue* it" which literally means to bring all of earth's resources under his power for the purpose of establishing the Kingdom of heaven on the planet. Adam used supernatural, "Subduing Knowledge and Authority" to fill the earth with the knowledge of the Glory of the Lord. The fall interrupted this plan! What the first Adam failed to do, the second Adam will finish. Follow me now... this is uncharted territory.

Jesus Christ came to planet earth to undo what the devil had done in 1 John 3:8. He came to loosen, undo and dissolve what the devil did in the garden and return to us the long lost Keys of the Kingdom of God (see Matt. 16:19). He shed His blood and rose again to redeem mankind and will come again one day to gather His church to an event in heaven called the marriage supper of the Lamb where we will be united with Him in marriage. After this is complete, Jesus Christ, the second Adam, will return again to this earth with His Bride and will set up His Millennial Reign in Jerusalem and rule the nations of the earth for a thousand years. Satan will also be bound for a thousand years. What do you think will be happening on planet earth? What I propose to you is this! Adam (Jesus Christ) and Eve (His bride, the church) will in effect be in full process of bringing healing and restoration to this fallen world and fulfill the original mandate that God gave Adam and Eve, to bring heaven to earth and fill it with the knowledge of the Glory of God. Revelation 22 is the very last book of the Bible and as a final note to all it reads:

> *THEN HE showed me the river whose waters give life, sparkling like crystal, flowing out from the throne of God and of the Lamb.*

*Through the middle of the broadway of the city; also, on either side of the river was the tree of life with its twelve varieties of fruit, yielding each month its fresh crop; **and the leaves of the tree were for the healing and the restoration of the nations** (Rev. 22:1-2).*

The nations are yet to be healed and restored! But this *River* that flowed in Genesis 2:8 in the beginning of time that brought life to the earth will flow once again out of the throne and of the Lamb that will bring healing and restoration to the nations of the earth.

John also heard and saw something else:

Then I heard a mighty voice from the throne and I perceived its distinct words, saying, See! The abode of God is with men, and He will live (encamp, tent) among them; and they shall be His people, and God shall personally be with them and be their God (Rev. 21:3).

There is coming a time after the marriage supper of the Lamb that the redeemed of the Lord shall return and make this planet look like Eden again. It will take 1,000 years to do so in our glorified bodies with the Messiah ruling from Jerusalem. God fully intended that Adam and Eve fill the earth with the knowledge of the Glory of God, establishing the Kingdom of God, pushing back darkness and extending the physical domain of heaven on earth through Adam and his Bride. I believe Jesus has plans for this planet and will return as the "Original or Second" Adam and finish the job!

BUILDING A BRAND NEW WORLD

The generation we live in is looking for something much greater than what the church has been offering it. They don't want to grow up to be like their mothers and fathers. They are a passionate generation looking for the real thing. It's not enough to tell them to give their lives to Jesus and hang on until we die and go to heaven. They need to know that they are being prepared for something much more glorious. They need to know that they will build a brand new world with Him and will live to rule nations on the earth. Not only that but the universe as well. The transformation of the earth is the beginning place. What about when the earth is completely transformed and the Kingdom of God has been expanded as far as it can be in the earth. What then? I'm telling you this is just the beginning! There are galaxies yet to be brought under the dominion of the Kingdom of God by us. This may be stretching some of you a bit but that's okay. We will have all of eternity to understand and do these things. But right now it's important that this generation understands that they are being fashioned for something much greater than to be just mere Christians that hold on until the return of Jesus. This is not enough for them. God has this all in mind. We will restore this whole planet! There is a future!

THE REDEEMED OF THE LORD SHALL RETURN

The commission for us here and now is to establish Kingdom authority on earth and to destroy the works of the devil like Jesus did.

> *The reason the Son of God was made manifest (visible) was to undo (destroy, loosen, and dissolve) the works the devil (has done)* (1 John 3:8).

The redeemed of the Lord shall return, making the wilderness pools of refreshing that the nations can come and be healed. I believe there will be worldwide revival before the Lord returns. The world is looking for the real Jesus Christ. They just haven't found Him represented yet in the church, but they will! In the Great Revival of all revivals they will say, "Oh, there's the Lord! We've been looking for Him." And, according to Isaiah 60:1, the nations will come to the brightness of our *rising*. The Lord will be seen in and through His people as they minister Kingdom power and authority like no other generation ever!

ARISE [from the depression and prostration in which circumstances have kept you--rise to a new life]! Shine (be radiant with the glory of the Lord), for your light has come, and the glory of the Lord has risen upon you! For behold, darkness shall cover the earth, and dense darkness [all] peoples, but the Lord shall arise upon you [O Jerusalem], and His glory shall be seen on you. And nations shall come to your light, and kings to the brightness of your rising (Isa. 60:1-3).

I hear the Lord saying to this generation, *"You see? I've raised you up, I've raised you to this place of joint seating, and I've put my words in your mouth, so speak. I've raised you up to release the sound of your voice into this place, so ask Me for the nations. I've raised you up into this place of ruling far above principalities and powers, far above dominion and authority so you could speak. So, ask me for the nations"* (see Eph. 2:6; Ps. 2:8).

When you are in that position and you have that place with the Lord, you have that authority, anointing, and revelation vibrating in your spirit man. In that place, the Lord says that you can ask Him anything in that day, and He will do it.

Does that mean you have to be perfect and sinless? Listen, we all stumble and fall—ask my wife, she'll be the first one to tell you—you don't have to be faultless and perfect, and cleaned up, you just have to simply understand your position and place and be humble and willing. That doesn't mean you quit practicing—I'm not saying that—but when you are in that place of understanding who you are, those chains will fall off. When you are in the presence of God, mindsets begin to shift and change. You find yourself being delivered, washed, and cleansed in the presence of God. It just happens as a byproduct—it's called sanctification.

How is God going to recreate this present world? I believe we are a BIG part of restoring all things. We are a major part of speaking, decreeing, and unleashing the government of God here on the earth, both now and in the reign to come.

And I have put My words in your mouth and have covered you with the shadow of My hand, that I may fix the [new] heavens as a tabernacle and lay the foundations of a [new] earth and say to Zion, You are My people (Isa. 51:16).

We are God's earthly ambassadors. We are the ones that implement His government on the planet. Psalm 116:15 says that *the heavens are the Lord's heavens, but the earth has He given to the children of men.*

The heavens belong to God. Heaven is God's throne; it was made for God, it was made for the spirit realm, it was made for the supernatural. Heaven belongs to God, but the dominion of earth He has given to man.

WE SHALL REIGN AS KINGS OVER THE EARTH

I've got news for you. Heaven is not the final destination for man throughout eternity. We will live on the new earth as well. As citizens of heaven will have a home in heaven, but will also play a part of living on planet earth and reframing and restoring it to its original design. God is going to build a brand new world down here. This may mess with the theology of some, but you need to look at the Scriptures. The Bible says that God will make a new heaven and a new earth, and that the New Jerusalem will descend out of heaven. Who is going to live on that new earth? We are! This is the ultimate expression of, *"On Earth as it is in Heaven."*

*And [now] they sing a new song, saying, You are worthy to take the scroll and to break the seals that are on it, for You were slain (sacrificed), and with Your blood You purchased men unto God from every tribe and language and people and nation. And You have made them a kingdom (royal race) and priests to our God, **and they shall reign [as kings] over the earth*** (Rev. 5:9-10)!

God is going to recreate and reframe this world and we are going to live on it. Like Adam, we will have dual citizenship and live both on the earth and have access to heaven. God is going to make the wilderness like Eden again as Jesus Christ *"the Second Adam"* and we His Bride *"the New Eve"* will together reframe and reconstitute planet earth. This was the original commission God gave Adam 6,000 years ago and it will ultimately be completed in the end.

Even now the Lord is beginning to Roar out of Zion through His church. It's our position, our place, and our right, as we rule with Kingdom authority on planet earth from the heavenly realm. The bottom line is this: I am family with God, and I do not owe my birth to my mother or father, but I owe my birth to God, I am born from another dimension. I am born from above.

> *Who owe their birth neither to bloods nor to the will of the flesh [that of physical impulse] nor to the will of man [that of a natural father], but to God. [They are born of God]* (John 1:13)!

Chapter 9

THE DREAD CHAMPIONS & END TIME ARMY OF GOD

BOB JONES 1979 VISION OF THE ARMY OF GOD

As all of us are already aware, we are in a season of great ups and downs in the nations of the earth. There are great uncertainties of our time which cause great tensions due to the lack of clarity for the future. At the same time we are in one of the most spiritually pivotal and progressive seasons we've been in for a long time. All can feel the spiritual tectonic plates ready to give way to a season of the new on many levels including revival. Wherever there are great tensions there is great power. All this being said there are prophetic meters that have been given to us to measure where we are at in these times through credible voices—and without a doubt, one of the most constant of these credible voices I know unarguably is Bob Jones. For many decades now, Bob Jones has accurately brought the Word of the Lord to churches, cities, regions and leaders globally with detailed accuracy. Before us there is a 30 year word from Bob that is getting ready to come to pass that I feel is most urgent—we need to hear it and understand it as it will encourage many. In short, here it is:

Back in January of 1979, the Lord took Bob into a vision to a place by the sea and called it the *"Sands of Time."* Bob said he saw great leaders, apostles and prophets that were representatives in their generations sticking their hands down into the sands to bring up what looked like old shoe boxes. As each one did, Bob could hear them say, *"Is this the time? ...Are the promises for now?"* With each of the leaders there was nothing in the box—as the promises weren't for their generation.

Then the Lord told Bob to reach down into the sands of time to pull up a box, but Bob said, *"Lord, they are all empty,"* but the Lord told Bob to open up the shoe box anyway. As Bob opened his box he was surprised to see draft notices in it. They said, *"Greetings, you have been drafted into the Army of God."*

Then the Lord told Bob, *"I will begin to send these letters out to my leaders when it costs twenty cents to mail a letter."* At the time of the vision, it cost only eleven cents to mail a letter so no one ever thought that the price would go up again. But on October 13, 1981, it cost twenty cents to mail a letter and the Lord said, *"Everyone that was conceived, that was in the womb, or nine months prior was literally the army of God. The first would be leaders and the second would be the greatest army that nothing could ever stop and when they reach the age of maturity I am going to begin to release them in power. I will arm them out of my armory in Heaven. There is no gift that I will deny them. They will literally pull down the warehouse of God and they will have no fear of the enemy. They will glorify me beyond anything that has ever been. They will represent me in my holiness and compassion."*

There is a new people group rising in the earth that is hungry for the Glory presence of God. They are not bound like much of the prior generations with the rules and regulations that have crippled, stunted or killed the post-modern church. This Army of God is hungry for the Kingdom of power and Glory.

THE AGE OF MATURITY

October 13, 1981 to October 13, 2011 will mark thirty years from the date.

The age of 30 is representative of the age of maturity. When Jesus was about to begin His public ministry he made His way to the river Jordan where John was baptizing. We know that Jesus is the Word of God for the Scriptures clearly tell us in John 1:1, *"In the beginning (before all time) was the Word (Christ), and the Word was with God, and the Word was God Himself."* And verses 10-11 state, *"He came into the world, and though the world was made through Him, the world did not recognize Him. He came to that which belonged to Him (to His own—His domain, creation, things, world) and they who were His own did not receive Him and did not welcome Him."*

As a young man growing up, Jesus grew in favor with both God and man. He was subjected to His mother and Joseph as long as He was under age. He was still a Son but was under the guidance of another and directly responsible to His guardians. This Greek word is called *Teknon*, which is a relationship formed between people by the bonds of love, friendship and trust, just as between parents and children. It is used in affectionate address by patrons, helpers, teachers, as if they are saying, "my child." Pupils and disciples are called "children" of their teachers, because the latter by their instruction nourish the minds of their pupils and mold their character.

This was the relationship with Jesus and His mother and the wedding feast in Galilee. They ran out of wine and Mary, Jesus' mother, told Him to do something about it. He told her plainly that it was not His time yet. Then, realizing that it was about to be His time of introduction to the world, she told the servants, "Whatever HE says, do it." It was no longer what she said. And this was the beginning of His public ministry. The time was at hand for Jesus' public ministry to begin. Suddenly, he found Himself at the river Jordan where John was baptizing.

In those days Jesus came from Nazareth of Galilee and was baptized by John in the Jordan. And when He came up out of the water, at once he [John] saw the heavens torn open and the [Holy] Spirit like a dove coming down [to enter] into Him. And there came a voice out from

*within heaven, You are My Beloved **Son**; in You I am well pleased.*
(Mark 1:9-11, emphasis mine).

The Greek word used here as "Son" is the word "Huios" which means "mature" or "full grown." When Jesus stepped down into the Jordan river He did as the Word of God, but yet a *Teknon* Son. Through the waters of baptism, He rose up and John saw the heavens torn open and the Holy Spirit like a dove coming down *to enter into Him* and *rest upon Him*. And there came a voice out of heaven saying, "You are My Beloved *Son* (Huios—Mature One) and in You I am well pleased.

This end time Army of God is coming of age in this season in preparation for what I believe will be one of the greatest revivals to ever sweep the world. Like Jesus did, they are reaching an "Age of Maturity" being baptized with both Word and the Spirit. He went down into the waters of baptism in the Jordan River as the Word of God and when He came up the Spirit of God filled Him and He became a Mature, *Huios*, Son of God. *Word and Spirit came together.* We've had many incredible moves of God in our day that

have impacted cities, states, regions and even nations, but there is coming a mature family of sons on the earth, a Glory generation that will be so filled with the Word and Spirit of God it will usher in the greatest end time revival the world will ever see.

Smith Wigglesworth prophesied in 1947 that the Great Revival would take place when two conditions were met. I want to quote this word in its entirety here in the following paragraphs.

SMITH WIGGLESWORTH

TWO DISTINCT MOVES

"During the next few decades there will be two distinct moves of the Holy

Spirit across the church in Great Britain. The first move will affect every church that is open to receive it and will be characterized by a restoration of the baptism and gifts of the Holy Spirit. The second move of the Holy Spirit will result in people leaving historic churches and planting new churches. In the duration of each of these moves, the people who are involved will say 'This is the great revival'. But the Lord says 'No, neither is this the great revival but both are steps towards it."

WORD AND SPIRIT

"When the new church phase is on the wane, there will be evidenced in the churches something that has not been seen before: a coming together of those with an emphasis on the Word and those with an emphasis on the Spirit.

When the Word and the Spirit come together, there will be the biggest movement of the Holy Spirit that the nation, and indeed the world, has ever seen. It will mark the beginning of a revival that will eclipse anything that has been witnessed within these shores, even the Wesleyan and the Welsh revivals of former years. The outpouring of God's Spirit will flow over from the UK to the mainland of Europe, and from there will begin a missionary move to the ends of the earth." [24]

Smith prophesied this in 1947. Since then we've seen the 1948 Latter Day Rain Revival; the 1950s Revival that swept the world; the Charismatic Renewal of the 1970s; Toronto Blessing of the 1990s, the Brownsville Revival; the Smithton Outpouring; and Lakeland outpouring with both Rodney Howard Brown and Todd Bentley. I believe this next move of God will be an outpouring of the very presence of God manifest in and through a Word-and-Spirit people. It will result in mass harvest and evangelism with corporate miracles, healings, signs and wonders never witnessed before. This will happen in and through a corporately anointed body of Christ on the earth filled with the Word and Spirit. The church is waking up. It's time for the dread champions to arise!

In *The Chronicles of Narnia*, many parallels reveal to us what the spiritual world is like. I was especially struck by a scene in the movie *Prince Caspian*. At the end of the story, Lucy has gone to find Aslan to help in the battle that was taking place against the enemies of Narnia. In a calm manner, Aslan states that it is time to "Wake up your old friends, the trees." Those trees were fearless and powerful in battle. Trees are symbolic of men. God is waking up the Lazarus generation who will be a generation of Mighty Ones on the earth at this time to will overthrow spiritual darkness on the earth. These are also known as the *Dread Champions of God*.

Let's look at the Book of Joel in the context of the "day of the Lord" and the "pouring out of the Spirit of God on all flesh in the last days." This supernatural army called the Mighty Ones are mentioned:

> *With a noise like chariots over mountaintops they leap, like the noise of a flaming fire that devours the stubble, like a strong people set in battle array. Before them the people writhe in pain; all faces are drained of color. They run like mighty men, they climb the wall like men of war; every one marches in formation, and they do not break ranks. They do not push one another; every one marches in his own column. Though they lunge between the weapons, they are not cut down. They run to and fro in the city, they run on the wall; they climb into the houses, they enter at the windows like a thief. The earth quakes before them, the heavens tremble; the sun and moon grow dark, and the stars diminish their brightness. The LORD gives voice before His army, for His camp is very great; for strong is the One who executes His word. For the day of the LORD is great and very terrible; who can endure it (Joel 2:5-11, NKJV)?*

A NEW BREED OF MIRACLE WORKER

There is a new breed of miracle worker coming to the forefront in these last days. They are the dread champions of God. These men and women will in many ways be like King David's mighty men who stand in unthinkable places and move with supernatural dimensions that the world has never seen. The church won't know what to do with them. Many of these will be unknown champions in the Glory and know the very presence of God. Jeremiah 20:11 reveals more about them: *"But the LORD is with me like a dread champion; therefore, my persecutors will stumble and not prevail. They will be utterly ashamed, because they have failed."*

Do you hear the battle alarm? It is ringing loud and clear! We are entering a very serious season—a season of confrontation. Our lukewarm "business as usual" attitude must die. The Spirit of God is awakening and arousing the Church, prompting us to arise and take a strong stand for Divine Truth. The war is raging and we must prepare for battle.

We are champions because we have overcome the world by the Blood of the Lamb and the word of our testimony; we are dread champions because we consider not our lives unto death. This level of radical obedience produces believers who will truly follow the Lamb wherever He goes—no matter the consequences.

This is the nature of a hero—and God is calling for spiritual heroes in this hour. The word *heroism* speaks of bravery and fearlessness. Heroes fight not for themselves, but for their King's honor, their country's honor, a greater honor than their own acclaim. These qualities of selfless valor are not born of the flesh, however. We cannot exert our will and abilities to become a dread champion. On the contrary, our heroism is in direct proportion to our yielding to Christ, the one true Hero. Only as we yield to the Holy Spirit will we be equipped to display these outstanding qualities of God's champions.

Arise and Be Bold as a Lion

Scripture declares in Proverbs 28:1, *"The wicked flee when no man pursues (them), but the righteous are as bold as a lion."* It is time to arise and shine!

Holy Scripture warns that, in the end times, the love of many will turn cold (see Matt. 24:12). We must not let the light of our hearts dim, but we are to be a shining beacon of hope and love, radiating God brightly in a sin-darkened world (see Matt. 5:14-16). If our light is to remain bright, however, we must rally now…. Now! We must embrace the call to become "keepers of the fire" and defend the flame of the Holy Spirit.

This is who you are now, beloved: you are a people of burning passion, standing strong and filled with true conviction—never cowering, no matter the persecution or attack. Although we are observing an all-out attack to undermine the foundation of the Church and our nation, you are called to burn brightly with passionate love and radical obedience, true to the King. This is the call of the dread champions.

Unleashing the Spirit of Revival

The sounds of revival can be heard in every generation, from the sound of a mighty, rushing wind on Pentecost, to the prayers of a young girl from Wales, Scotland that launched the great Welch revival, to Azusa Street, to the Latter Rain outpouring, Cain Ridge Revival, Jansenists, Hugenots, to the more modern, healing revivalists like Maria Woodworth Etter, they all had a sound.

What sound do we carry? I believe it is yet to be seen. However, whenever God moved, it was with the sound of a roar, the sound of a people who were His.

There is much being talked about in this season of time in the church as well as in the secular arena about the year 2012. Documentaries have been made from the History channel to Discovery Channel and beyond surrounding a pending shift coming to the earth. Some say it's the literal end of the world, others are saying it's the end of the world as we know it, but all agree on one thing: change is coming to the planet.

Many are speculating that a doomsday of sorts will hit the planet in the form of an asteroid, or earthquake or some other form of calamity. All of this is centered around dates given by specific people groups from thousands of years ago, all of whom are not connected in anyway shape, fashion or form.

The Mayan civilization was known for their unique ability to accurately predict events according to the solar and lunar calendar. The Mayan calendar is a system of calendars and almanacs used in the Maya civilization of pre-Columbian Mesoamerica, and in some modern Maya communities in highland Guatemala and Oaxaca, Mexico. The essentials of the Maya calendar system are based upon a system that had been in common use throughout the region, dating back to at least the 5th century BCE.

Mayan civilization, known for advanced writing, mathematics and astronomy, flourished for centuries in Meso-America, especially between A.D. 300 and 900. Its Long Count calendar, which was discontinued under Spanish colonization, tracks more than 5,000 years, then resets at year zero.

Part of the 2012 mystique stems from the stars. On the winter solstice in 2012, the sun will be aligned with the center of the Milky Way for the first time in about 26,000 years. The Solstice on December 21, 2012, precisely at 11:11 am Universal time, marks the completion of the 5,125 year Great Cycle of the Ancient Maya Long Count Calendar. Rather than being a linear end-point, this cycle that is closing is naturally followed by the start of a new cycle. What this new cycle has in store for humanity is what many call a mystery that has yet to unfold.

THE SUPER SHIFT

The Scriptures teach us that the heavens declare the Glory of God. Long before Astronomers and Astrologists were noted for the study of the stars,

God had a cosmic timetable embedded in the universe that would keep perfect time and foretell the coming of great events. Daniel along with astrologists from his time knew these things as he accurately portrayed the coming of Messiah in numbers of days. The "wise men" who came seeking Jesus from the far east were astrologers that knew the times and the season of the coming of this heavenly King that was to be born in Bethlehem because of Daniel's understanding of the cosmic calendar. They came looking for a "star" and were guided to the Christ by that star in the heavens. That Cosmic revelation ushered in a Super Shift in humanity that resulted in the redemption of mankind by the blood of Jesus Christ, the second Adam. This Super Shift was the beginning of a new cycle and the New Testament of the church. The government of God came to the earth and an era of power and revelation was ushered into the church. All of this happened by the heavens declaring it. All of this happened within the understanding of God's Cosmic calendar.

Job 38:31-33 talks about the signs of the Zodiac in the heavens:

> *Can you bind the chains of [the cluster of stars called] Pleiades, or loose the cords of [the constellation] Orion? 32Can you lead forth the signs of the zodiac in their season? Or can you guide [the stars of] the Bear with her young? Do you know the ordinances of the heavens? Can you establish their rule upon the earth?*

1 Chronicles 12:32 says that the sons of Issachar were men who had understanding of the times to know what Israel should do. They were men who had a revelation of the times and seasons who knew what God was saying and were able to communicate this to the house of Israel.

GOD'S COSMIC CALENDAR

I believe that the heavens are like a cosmic calendar that foretells all that God has in store for us. Even science has found this to be true and to be accurate right down to the exact second. The early Mayan civilization knew this as well as other civilizations and were able to accurately count and predict times and seasons with astounding accuracies. As this relates to the 2012 date, I believe that the heavens are definitely portraying a point of demarcation coming to the planet. Many see it and are speculating what this all means. The new age community sees it as a shift in upper consciousness that will propel mankind into a God like state of being. I definitely don't believe this, however there is something foreshadowed by the hand of God that is getting the attention of the world.

I believe we are moving into a Super Shift in the body of Christ that will unlock mysteries to the Kingdom of God in ways the church has never seen before. Just as the heavens declared the coming of Jesus Christ, the second Adam would come and be the first born among many brothers, so I believe that the Church of Jesus Christ is being prepared to usher in a second coming of the Lord Jesus Christ with incredible miracles, healings, signs and wonders. I personally believe that we are in a place in human history in which great mysteries are being revealed by revelation knowledge. The blinders that have been upon the corporate church will no longer be able to sustain their obstruction, as revelation and understanding will propel the church forward. She will know *the power of Christ in us—the hope of Glory*. The occult sees this paradigm shift coming but the Church seems to be blind to it. God always reveals in the heavens first what He is going to reveal on the earth.

2012 THE YEAR OF MAN

Bob Jones was shown a vision about the years 2009 to 2012. He saw 2009 was the year of plowing or the year of the Ox. 2010 was the year of the eagle. 2011 is the year of the Lion where great keys of authority have been given the church to unlock the new realms of the Kingdom of God. Those keys unlock the power the enemy and power over the natural realm. We have passed the year of the roaring of the Lion of the Tribe of Judah. But the year 2012 is the year of the face of the Man. It's in this season that all four of these faces will begin to move together ushering in the mobile throne of God. Ezekiel saw this vision in Ezekiel chapters 1 and 2. The Throne of God moved with eyes and wings, wheels within wheels moving where the Spirit of the Lord moved it. Like Bob Jones, I believe 2012 is the beginning of what many are seeing of a release of Kingdom authority on the earth that trumps any other era or age before it.

A NEW BREED OF SUPER HUMANS

The heavens are declaring this Super Shift now, and we are going to witness a coming forth of an anointed people group that move in the upper realms of revelation and power being prepared to bring in and end time a harvest of souls! They will not do this by conventional means but by a new breed of super humans, moving with supernatural ability and looking just like their older brother, Jesus Christ. Jesus paid the ultimate price in blood to produce from seed form what will be revealed in these last days as a mature bride that has grown and developed throughout the last 2,000 years. He is the first born among many brothers or those who look like the Original Seed. And this company will do the same miracles and greater to reveal the true nature of God in the earth.

FURIOUS SOUND OF GLORY CONCLUSION

This book, *The Furious Sound of Glory*, is a clarion call to an end time church to rise from slumber into a glorious end time church that moves in the same miracles Jesus did. At the end of the age it is clear there is a great harvest of souls coming in. This harvest will be brought in by a supernatural generation that has been thoroughly prepared for harvest. This many-membered, corporately anointed Body of Christ will do the same miracles Jesus did 2,000 years ago. We are His Body and He will reap the reward to His suffering. The Lord will Roar out of Zion and the harvest will come in. Get ready. This is the season, now is the time and we are the generation through which the Lord Jesus Christ will release The Furious Sound of Glory.

1. Sound of Heaven Symphony of Earth, Ray Hughes, Page 17
2. The Singing God by Timothy J. Joyce, OSB, STL, December 25, 2009, Glastonbury Abbey
3. Does a singing God have relevance in our world?, The Elegant Universe, Brian Greene, www.pbs.org/wgbh/nova/elegant/resonance.html
4. Glory Rising, Jeff Jansen, 2009, Destiny Image Publishers, Shippensburg, PA, 114
5. The Science of God Sound, Article, David Van Koevering: http://www.davidvankoevering.com
6. The Singing River by M. Keith Hudson, Wildlife Biologist, Alabama Division of Wildlife and Freshwater Fisheries
7. Physics of the Supernatural Realm, Article, David Van Koevering: http://www.davidvankoevering.com
8. Forerunner, Charles Whitaker, "Ready Answer," July 1998
9. Power from on High, Charles G. Finney, Christian Literature Crusade, Fort Washington
10. God's Generals: The Revivalists, Roberts Liardon, 2008, Whitaker House, 109
11. Ibid., 111
12. Ibid., 114
13. God's Generals: Why They Succeeded Why Some Failed, Roberts Liardon, 1996, Whitaker House, 45 - 76
14. Ibid., 45 - 76
15. Ibid., 317
16. Ibid., 319
17. Sound of Heaven Symphony of Earth, Ray Hughes, Page 19
18. Sound Barrier, Wikipedia: http://en.wikipedia.org/wiki/Sound_barrier
19. Glory Rising, Jeff Jansen, 2009, Destiny Image Publishers, Shippensburg, PA, 126
20. Ibid., 209
21. Author: David El-Cana Bryan; 2011 Questions and/or concerns regarding this amazing true story can be directed to me and Cheryl at info@ChurchOfGladTidings.com
22. Revelation, Faith and Matter, Audio Teaching, Renny McLain: http://www.globalglory.org
23. The Science of God Sound, Article, David Van Koevering: http://www.davidvankoevering.com
24. http://www.jonasclark.com/revival-history/smith-wigglesworths-rare-1947-prophecy.html

About Jeff Jansen

Jeff Jansen is an internationally known conference speaker and crusade evangelist. Jeff is also Founder of Global Fire Ministries International, and Senior Pastor of the Global Fire Church and World Miracle Center located in Murfreesboro, Tennessee.

These ministries include;

- Global Fire Church & World Miracle Center
- Global Fire TV
- Global Fire International Crusades
- Global Fire Covenant Network (A Fellowship of Church)
- Global Fire Kingdom Life Institute (School of Supernatural Ministry)
- Global Fire Prayer Furnace (10 state Regional Revival Meetings)

Jeff's burning desire is to see churches, cities, regions and whole nations ignited and transformed by the power of God. Jeff flows in a strong prophetic and miracle healing anointing that releases the tangible Glory of God everywhere he goes. Jeff also teaches, trains and equips believers how to live and move in the supernatural presence of God and emphasizes that communion and intimacy with the Holy Spirit is vital for transformation. Jeff believes that the same Holy Spirit that rested in and upon Jesus Christ then is the same Spirit that flows in and through the corporate body of Christ now, and that we are to be equipped and released as Kingdom Ambassadors to the nations of the earth. Global Fire Ministries in an inter-denominational ministry aimed at equipping and igniting the Body of Christ for Global harvest.

Jeff, his wife Jan and family live in Nashville, Tennessee area.

Contact

Global Fire Ministires
325 Walla Court
Murfreesboro, TN 37128

website: www.globalfireministries.com
email: info@globalfireministries.com
twitter: @jeff_jansen

Global Fire Creations

visit our website at: www.globalfirecreations.com

RECEIVE A FREE GIFT

Subscribe to our e-newsletter and receive a
free downloadable gift
visit: www.globalfireministries.com to subscribe

To Purchase Additional

Global Fire Creations

Products visit: www.globalfirestore.com

GLOBAL FIRE SCHOOL OF SUPERNATURAL MINISTRY

GET STARTED TODAY!

Intimacy - Identity - Destiny

9 Month Intensive Ministry Training School.

Founder: Jeff Jansen   Overseer: Eric Green

Endorsed By:

Bob Jones
Larry Randolph
James Goll
Patricia King
Ray Hughes
Bobby Conner
Jake Hamilton
Ryan Wyatt
Jerame & Miranda Nelson

Visit www.kingdomlifeinstitute.com
for more information.

ALSO AVAILABLE
From the Global Fire Store

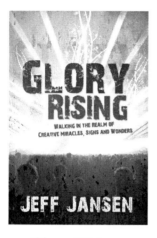

Other Books by Jeff Jansen

Glory Rising,

Glory Rising Manual,

Adventures in the Prophetic,

School of the Holy Spirit,

*Supernatural School of Miracles, Healing,
Impartation & Activation,*

Revival of the Secret Place